Historic
Motor Cycles

Historic
Motor Cycles
David Burgess Wise

Hamlyn
London · New York · Sydney · Toronto

My special thanks are due to Paul Foulkes-Halbard, who gave me the freedom of his library and wheeled out his magnificent TT Indian for the artist; to Norman Aubury of the Cycle & Motor Cycle Manufacturers' Association, who provided an enormous pile of documents on the two-wheeler industry; and to Arthur Bourne ('Torrens' of *Motor Cycle*), who gave me my first writing job . . .

The drawings throughout the book were prepared by Terry Dutton of Whitecroft Designs, and for photographs I am grateful to D. Dixon, the Hamlyn Group Library, David Hodges, the editor of *Motor Cycle*, the Smithsonian Institution, Desmond Tripp, Benn White and Mick Woollett.

DBW

Published by the Hamlyn Publishing Group Limited
London · New York · Sydney · Toronto
Astronaut House, Feltham, Middlesex, England
Copyright © The Hamlyn Publishing Group Limited, 1973

ISBN 0 600 34407 X

Text set in 'Monophoto' Plantin
by London Filmsetters Limited
Printed in Great Britain by Sir Joseph Causton and Sons Limited

Contents

Steam and Hot Air

The origins of the motor cycle are shrouded in mystery; the first suggestion for a self-propelled two-wheeler appeared in the form of a caricature in 1818 under the imposing portmanteau title of 'Velocipedraisiavaporianna'. The print claimed to depict 'a very surprising *mécaeonomique* invented in Germany which was demonstrated in the Jardin du Luxembourg, Paris, on Sunday April 5, 1818'; the machine did not in fact exist. The drawing was a satire on a crude ancestor of the bicycle, the Draisienne, which was powered only by the rider's feet pressing against the ground.

However, it was a brilliant if unintentional prophecy (the application of cranks to the driving wheel was not adopted for several decades), which claimed that, should the horse become extinct, it would be replaced by steam motor cycles.

A decade later, cartoonists were again featuring motor cycles—Alken, Aitken and Leech all drew little one-man tricycles and quadricycles in their vision of a

steam-powered future, and there are grounds for believing that these drawings were based on fact, for by that time steam carriages were in limited service on the roads of England. The technical skills of the day would have been capable of producing engines small and powerful enough for the purpose, and the similarity of the machines in the various prints seems to point to an existing prototype.

The first motor cycle of which definite proof exists appeared 40 years later, in 1867 when, it is claimed, Ernest Michaux, pioneer of the pedal-driven bicycle, fitted a light steam engine to one of his velocipedes. The next year, in December, one Perreaux patented a steam motor cycle, which was basically a Michaux velocipede with a single-cylinder engine which had a petroleum burner, mounted beneath the saddle and driving the rear wheel through twin belts.

Meanwhile, the velocipede had been introduced to the New World by Pierre Lallement, an ex-Michaux man, who claimed that he had invented the pedal drive in 1861, and his employer had merely filched the idea. In 1868 the first American motor cycle appeared, built by Silvester Roper.

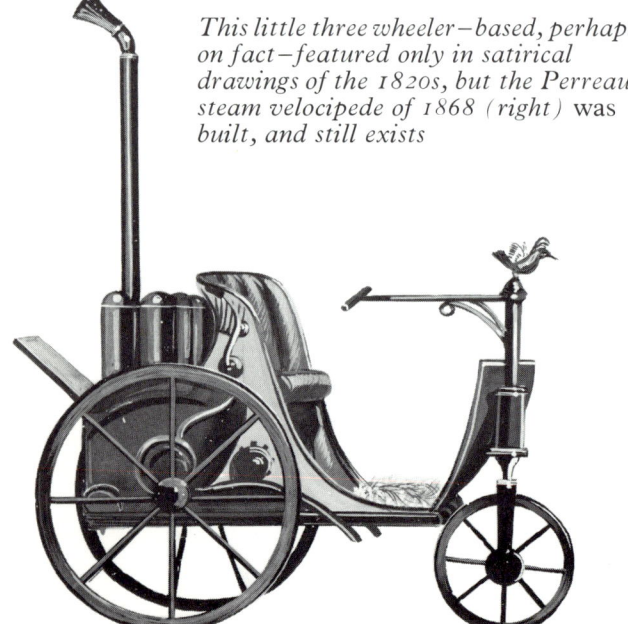

This little three wheeler—based, perhaps, on fact—featured only in satirical drawings of the 1820s, but the Perreaux steam velocipede of 1868 (right) was built, and still exists

Early Americana – Silvester Roper's 1868 velocipede (above) and Lucius Copeland's delicate Phaeton Motorcycle 'with Amaryllis in the shade' outside the Smithsonian Institution, Washington, in 1888

The Roper machine had a twin-cylinder engine, with a cylinder either side of the velocipede's backbone, driving cranks on the back axle directly with the connecting rods. The coal-fired boiler hung between the wheels, and there was a raked funnel behind the saddle. Roper is said to have built around ten steam velocipedes and buggies, which he exhibited at fairs and circuses. He dropped dead, apparently from a heart attack, on June 1 1896, while demonstrating one of his bicycles on the Charles River cycle track at Cambridge, Massachusetts.

A key figure in the development of the steam motor cycle was Lucius Copeland, of Phoenix, Arizona. In 1881 he attempted to fix an auxiliary engine to a Columbia high-wheel bicycle, discarded the idea as 'inefficient and dangerous' and proceeded to design an ultra-light power unit for his 'farthing-penny' Star bicycle.

By 1884 the machine was ready. A diminutive boiler fed the engine (said to have weighed no more than 18lb complete) which drove a huge pulley on the rear wheel via a belt. The cycle could attain around 12mph.

Copeland sought backers, and in 1887 formed the Northrop Manufacturing Co., of Camden, New Jersey, in association with Sanford Northrop and two doctors, Starkey and Palen. Within three months, Copeland had a reliable three-wheeled 'Phaeton Moto-Cycle' on the road. A two-seated steam 'safety cycle' appeared in 1888. Later, a third wheel was added on an outrigger, carrying another saddle, the first germ of the sidecar idea.

Some 200 Moto-Cycles are optimistically claimed to have been made, and by 1890 the design had become quite sophisticated, with a range of 30 miles at 10mph, and the ability to start from cold in 5 minutes.

However, Copeland had become convinced that there was no money to be made from cars, and retired from the scene, leaving steam motor cycles mainly to amateur engineers including, apparently the aviation pioneers, Wilbur and Orville Wright. But the Kentish

firm of Pearson & Cox produced 'quite a few' steam bicycles in 1912–14.

Back in France, a single-cylinder steam motor cycle had been built in 1870 by Chapuis Frères.

Perhaps the most persistent experimenter was the Scottish amateur James Sadler, who cremated four pairs of trousers during trials of his speedy 1926 one-off,

Copeland's first successful steam cycle was this 'Star' highwheeler of 1884. It was capable of a breakneck 12mph

Daimler's 1885 two-wheeled test bed (above) was a crude makeshift, but Butler's three-wheeler of the same year (right) was a polished design, which was stifled by restrictive laws

as well as scorching bystanders' eyebrows. He was still trying in 1940 . . .

One of the first attempts at building a bicycle powered by an alternative to a steam engine was made in 1882 by R. W. Brownhill of Walsall, Staffordshire, who proposed fitting a piston and air reservoir to a two-wheeler, so that 'when descending a hill air can be compressed into the reservoir, and the power thus obtained utilised for driving the vehicle up the next hill'. Not surprisingly, this scheme proved impracticable.

However, only a year later, in Germany, Gottleib Daimler and his associate Wilhelm Maybach, succeeded in producing the first high-speed four-stroke internal combustion engine, which ran at a giddy 700–900 rpm, compared with the contemporary gas-engine's sluggardly 180 rpm. In 1885 Daimler constructed, purely as a test-bench, a crude wooden-framed two-wheeler, with two outrigged steady wheels, powered by an air-cooled 267 cc engine developing 0·5 bhp. As a bicycle, it was 20 years out of date, and once it had served its purpose Daimler discarded it for the horseless carriage (the company he founded never built another motor cycle).

The three-wheeler designed by an Englishman, Edward Butler, was much more advanced. Drawings of the machine were exhibited at the 1884 Stanley Bicycle Show, and the tricycle was completed and running the following year.

The Butler Tricycle was a remarkable design by any standards. Its four-stroke engine had two cylinders mounted horizontally – one either side of the single rear wheel. Curious curved connecting rods passed over the cylinders linking the forward-pointing piston rods with cranks on the rear wheel, driving the machine through a 6:1 epicyclic reduction gear. Advanced features of the vehicle were electric ignition (Daimler

used an incandescent metal tube heated by a petrol burner) and the earliest known float-feed spray carburetter, similar in principle to the units fitted to modern machines. The rotary valves were driven by chain from the rear wheel, and the petrol/air mixture was pre-heated before it entered the cylinders. Water for cooling the engine was carried in the hollow rear mudguard. Before starting the engine, the rider depressed a 'clutch' pedal which forced two small wheels down on the ground, jacking up the rear wheel. Once the engine was running the wheel was lowered again, enabling the tricycle to move away. Hand levers on either side of the driving seat operated the steering.

Butler designed another machine with vertical cylinders, but this was never built, as he lacked the capital to develop his motor tricycles further, and in any case the contemporary anti-motoring laws made such machines impracticable. The steam tricycles designed by Sir Thomas Parkyns (one was still running

In 1893 the Italian engineer Bernardi built this 'power trailer' which could be bolted to an ordinary pedal cycle – the forerunner of the 'clip-on' engine

in the early 1900s) and by S. Beeney of Birmingham in the late 1880s were also legislated off the roads.

Butler's assistant, C. T. Crowden, later played a prominent part in the early days of the motor industry, as works manager to the Great Horseless Carriage Company.

Another advanced British design was the two-stroke oil-engined tricycle built by J. D. Roots in 1892. This had the engine mounted crankcase uppermost behind the rear axle, which it drove through bevel gearing. Behind the steering head was a radiator, and cooling water circulated through the frame tubes. The air/oil mixture was sucked into the cylinder through a non-return valve and preheated before it entered the combustion chamber. Ignition was by hot tube on the Daimler system.

This machine apparently ran quite successfully at low speeds and a limited number of an improved four-stroke version was sold, mainly to French customers, leading to the manufacture of the celebrated Roots & Venables heavy oil cars from 1894.

The year 1892 also saw the appearance of the first really successful motor cycle, which was built in Munich by two German engineers, Hildebrand and Wolfmuller. They had experimented with steam bicycles in the late 1880s before turning to the internal combustion engine.

The Hildebrand & Wolfmuller design, which went into full production in 1894, had a 1487cc flat twin engine driving directly on to cranks on the rear axle. It weighed 112lb and had a maximum speed of 28mph.

Two noteworthy features of the design were a throttle control on the handlebars—this did not become standard practice for many years—and a dropped frame, so that in theory the machine was suitable for riders of either sex.

The design was built under licence in France as *La Pétrolette* by Duncan, Superbie et Cie. At its peak the firm was said to have employed 1200 workmen, but by

The first volume-produced motor cycle was the Hildebrand & Wolfmuller of 1894–97 (below)
In the primitive surface carburetter (above, right) petrol, vapourised by the jolting of the machine plus warmth from the exhaust, mixed with air sucked down the vertical chimney, passed into a barrel throttle and then into the engine. Most controls of the early motor cycle (right) were mounted on the fuel tank—gas and air levers, the exhaust lifter and the ignition advance. Only the on/off ignition switch was on the handlebars, incorporated in the left-hand grip

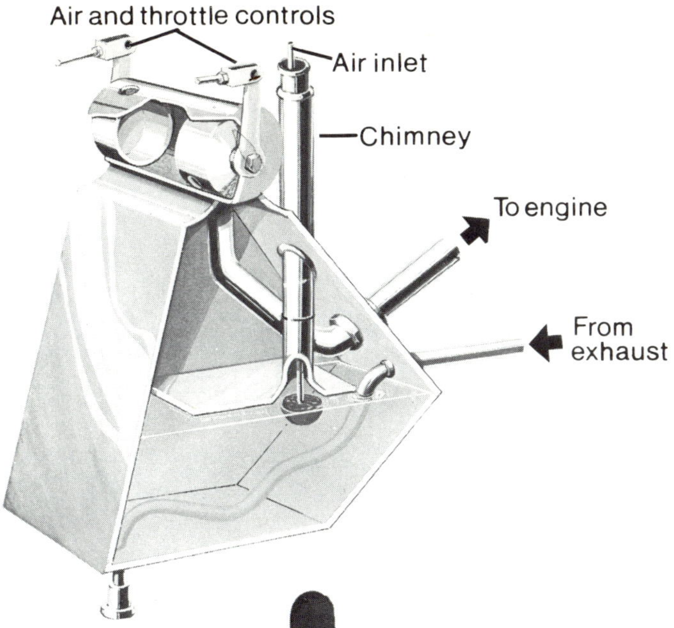

Air and throttle controls

Air inlet

Chimney

To engine

From exhaust

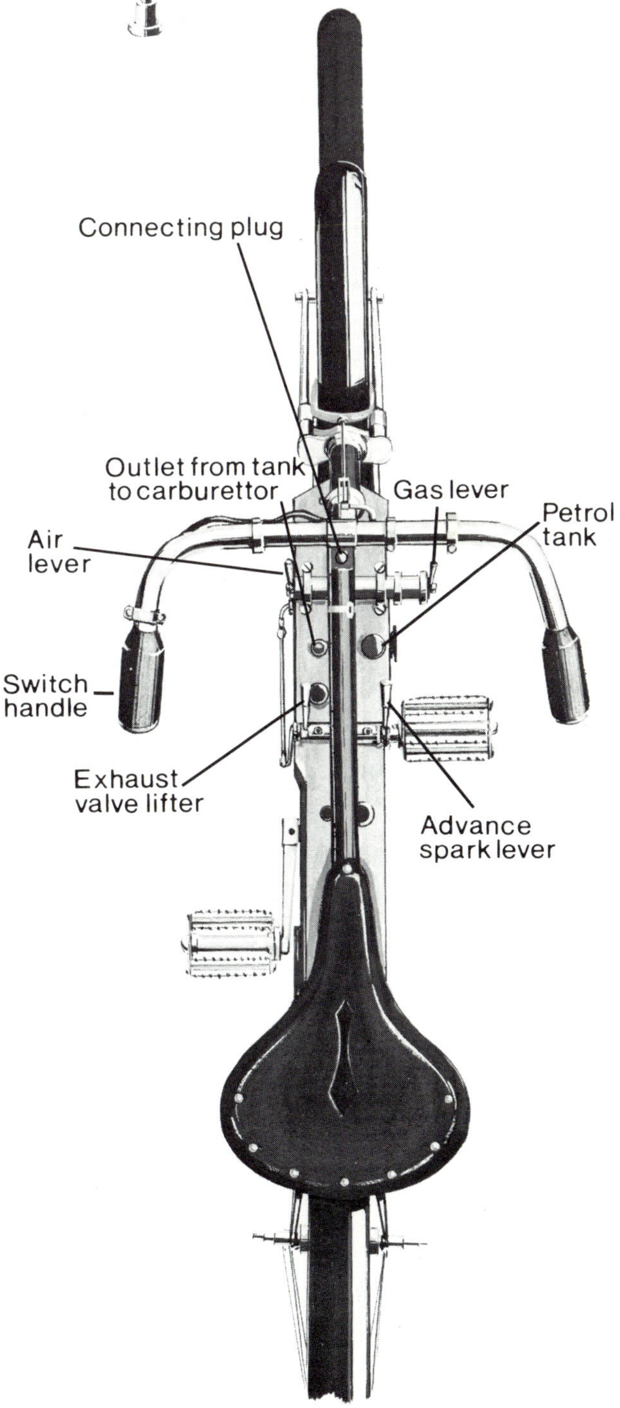

Connecting plug

Outlet from tank to carburettor

Gas lever

Petrol tank

Air lever

Switch handle

Exhaust valve lifter

Advance spark lever

The first De Dion tricycle of 1895 had a 120cc engine mounted behind the rear axle; it was soon developed for racing

1897 commercial pressures had forced the Hildebrand off the market.

Contemporary with the Hildebrand was the Millet, another petrol design based on steam experience. Built by a firm controlled by Alexandre Darracq, the Millet had a five-cylinder rotary engine built into the rear wheel: a contemporary writer noted acidly, 'It was not very successful'.

Both Hildebrand and Millet machines competed in the 1895 Paris–Bordeaux–Paris motor race. Their performances were so poor that M. Collin, deputed to report on the event to the French Institute of Civil Engineers, decided that the motor bicycle was doomed to remain a curiosity, and that even single-seated vehicles would always need four wheels.

But even as M. Collin wrote, the De Dion tricycle, the machine which above all others established the motor cycle industry, was making its first impact on the market. The firm of De Dion, Bouton and Trépardoux which had been founded in 1882, was an unlikely alliance between the portly Marquis de Dion, a pillar of Parisian society, Georges Bouton, a tiny moustachioed mechanic, and his brother-in-law, Trépardoux. Bouton and Trépardoux had originally been makers of showcase models—*modèles de vitrine* (often mistranslated as steam engines with cylinders of glass)—and the quality of their workmanship had brought them to the notice of De Dion, who planned to build a light steam-carriage.

During the 1880s the partnership's steam tricycles went into limited production, but in 1889 De Dion and Bouton were so impressed by the Daimler petrol engines and horseless carriages displayed at the Paris Exhibition that they decided to develop their own internal combustion power-unit.

Trépardoux, a steam enthusiast to the core, was con-

vinced that they were wasting their time: in 1894 he resigned in protest.

The following year Bouton produced a 120cc engine rated at only half a horsepower, yet capable of the unprecedented speed of 1800rpm, 'which surprised its inventor'.

This diminutive power-unit was mounted behind the axle of a pedal tricycle, driving the rear axle through exposed bevel gearing. A surface carburettor was fitted, a metal cylinder in which the volatile petrol then obtainable was persuaded to evaporate and form a combustible mixture simply by the jolting it received as the unsprung tricycle jolted and rattled along the unmade roads of the day. The speed of the tricycle could be regulated to some extent by advancing or retarding the electric ignition.

Despite obvious imperfections in its design, the Dion tricycle soon became extremely popular. The marque won several racing victories, and a De Dion engine (or a Chinese copy of one) became an essential of the good, moderately-priced, light motor vehicle.

But as power outputs increased, one major drawback of the original De Dion layout became apparent: there was so much weight behind the axle and so little in front that it was almost possible to tip a machine over backwards by pulling with one finger hooked below the nose of the saddle.

Other makers tried other means of eliminating this tendency to 'hydroplane', Renaux for example slinging the engine horizontally below the pedalling gear.

The first four-cylinder motor cycle appeared in 1895, with a water-cooled engine with cylinders in opposed pairs. The connecting rods, driving direct on the rear axle, acted on crosshead pins projecting from slots in the cylinder walls. This was the brainchild of Colonel

'The Renaux Motor', claimed the makers in 1900, 'is placed right on the centre line of the tricycle and low down; this arrangement brings the explosion chamber and valve box to the front, so that it meets fully the current of air caused by the forward motion of the tricycle. This disposition of the Motor also makes the tricycle much stronger, and by keeping the centre of gravity low, there is no fear of the tricycle being upset. The vibration of the Motor is not felt to anything like the same extent as with a vertically placed motor'

The exhaust of the Holden four-cylinder motor cycle was led through the petrol tank to warm the fuel and assist carburation. The result was a machine that ran smoothly, except at low speeds

This curious three-wheeler was the first motor vehicle built by Rover, in 1899. It was a mechanised bathchair with a De Dion engine

H.C.L.Holden, a brilliant engineer who later designed the Brooklands race track. For various reasons production did not get under way seriously until 1901, by which time the design was outdated, despite the optimistic tone affected in their advertising by the manufacturers, the Motor Traction Co. of London.

'The year 1902 will be a MOTOR BICYCLE YEAR', they claimed.

'The motors at present used in bicycles are of 1–2hp, air cooled and drive by band or gear.

The Motor Bicycle for 1902 is The HOLDEN.

3bhp motor, water-cooled (no pumps).

Direct Driving (no belts, bands or gearing).

Four cylinders (no jerk or jar).

Cushioned Reciprocating Action (smooth running).

Automatic Lubrication (for 120 miles), all control on handlebar.

The action is steady, automatically cushioned and very smooth and even, therefore eliminating a tendency to sideslip, so noticeable in bicycles not so constructed.

No pedalling is necessary at any time, not even on steep hills'.

In Britain in the 1890s, when the law still compelled a man to walk in front of any motor vehicle, progress in all aspects of motoring was almost negligible, despite pioneers like Roots and Holden. So Sir David Salomans, a wealthy motoring enthusiast, organised a demonstration of horseless carriages at Tunbridge Wells in Kent, in October 1895. Among the spectators was one man who saw the potential of the stuttering machines in the arena.

Harry John Lawson was 33, and the son of a Brighton clergyman. He had entered the cycle trade in the 1870s, and, together with a mechanic named James Likeman, had patented one of the earliest designs for a safety bicycle.

Lawson was not a practical engineer – his ability lay in exploiting the inventions of others – which soon led him into the shadier side of company promotion under the wing of the egregious Terah Hooley, whose name became a byword for the flotation of grossly over-capitalised companies. In 1880 Lawson was general manager of the Rudge Cycle Company of Coventry, where he designed, and almost certainly built, a cycle powered by 'compressed gas'.

By the early 1890s the cycle boom was showing signs of imminent collapse, while the motor vehicle promised ripe pickings for the future. Lawson's first move was to acquire the British patent rights for the two most practical Continental engines, the Daimler and the De Dion, and any other workable designs, so that once a relaxation in the law stimulated interest in motor vehicles in Britain, he would hold the whiphand over any would be manufacturers.

Late in 1895 Lawson formed the British Motor Syndicate, followed in January 1896 by the Daimler Motor Company. Manufacture of Anglicised Panhard-Levassor cars began in a disused cotton factory, re-christened the Motor Mills.

Then he had a De Dion tricycle sent to Accles Limited of Birmingham, who copied the power unit, but modified the frame design so that the engine was ahead of the rear axle.

One prototype was built with De Dion electric ignition, but since the mysteries of the electric fluid were apparently beyond the contemporary British motor engineer, the dangerous and retrograde step of fitting hot-tube ignition was taken. About a thousand of these engines were built. Among the machines fitted with this power unit was the Coventry Motette lady's bicycle, which featured friction drive by a wooden pulley rubbing on the rear tyre. One of these cycles was ridden from Coventry to London by Mrs F.H.de Veulle, who was presented with a diamond ring by Lawson for the feat. She thoroughly earned the reward, for the lopsided layout of the machine meant that the flaming ignition burner – and the petrol tank – was almost beneath her saddle!

Another project, masterminded by Lawson and his associate Charles McRobie Turrell, was the Coventry Motette, a modified version of the French Léon Bollée three-wheeled *voiturette* (the famous racing cyclist S.F.Edge started his motoring career on a Bollée purchased from Lawson, going on to become a leading racing driver and the power behind the Napier car).

In May 1896, with repeal of the restrictive Locomotives on Highways Act only six months away, Lawson organised an exhibition in London's Imperial Institute at which both cars and motor cycles were demonstrated.

At this point in the saga a colourful crook named Edward Joel Pennington breezed into the Lawson orbit from America, where he was known as Airship Pennington after a dubious flying machine project of 1890. Pennington had constructed, around 1894–95, a singularly crude 'moto-cycle' with long drainpipe cylinders devoid of cooling, drip fuel feed instead of a carburettor and the mysterious 'long-mingling spark', which was said to enable the machine to run on paraffin. However, best petrol was always used, the paraffin claim only being upheld with the aid of a faked densimeter. Advertisements showed this cycle (reputedly capable of 65mph) vaulting a wide river, and on the strength of this fictitious feat and some unlikely prototypes–including a propellor-driven bicycle displayed at the 1896 National Cycle Show–Pennington unloaded the British rights to his patents on to Lawson for £100 000–of which £90 000 was in cash.

Largely on the strength of Pennington's designs, Lawson floated the Great Horseless Carriage Company, also based at the Motor Mills, and capitalised for £1 000 000.

Although large numbers of Pennington moto-cycles were ordered, only two were built, made by Humber at their Ford Street works in Coventry, before the premises were destroyed by fire in 1896.

The Penningtons were far from successful. T. W. Blumfield, who helped to build the machines, and who actually rode them, recalled: 'The machine would run from about 8 or 10 miles an hour, its slowest speed, to about 30 miles an hour. There being no compression release or exhaust valve lifter, and the bore and stroke being $2\frac{1}{2}$in by 6in, the difficulties of slow running can be imagined.

Although the cylinders were not normally cooled in any way, overheating was not one of the troubles experienced, and it ran as far as, perhaps, 10 miles without a breakdown, though on most occasions the ignition failed very quickly and a new spring wiper had to be fitted'.

The failure of Pennington's designs was a major cause of the slump which hit the British motor cycle industry in the late 1890s and early 1900s. It also proved to be the first nail in the coffin of the Lawson empire, which collapsed in ruins around 1900. However, the irrepressible Pennington turned up again shortly before his death in 1911, claiming £108 000 from the Hendee company, makers of the Indian Motocycle on the grounds of infringement of his 'basic patent' for motor cycles.

Rather more success was enjoyed by the Werner Motocyclette, the brainchild of two emigré Russian journalists living in Paris, the brothers Eugene and Michel Werner. They had already tried–and failed–to make their fortune from phonographs and typewriters, when in 1897 they turned to the motor cycle as the coming thing.

Their Motocyclette answered the need for basic transportation, having a $\frac{3}{4}$hp air-cooled engine mounted

This solo Pennington moto-cycle was capable of jumping a 65 foot wide river as part of its everyday work! Or so the company's advertising claimed . .

The original Werner was a 'demon for sideslip', although the substitution of electric for hot-tube ignition reduced the risk of fire when the machine overturned

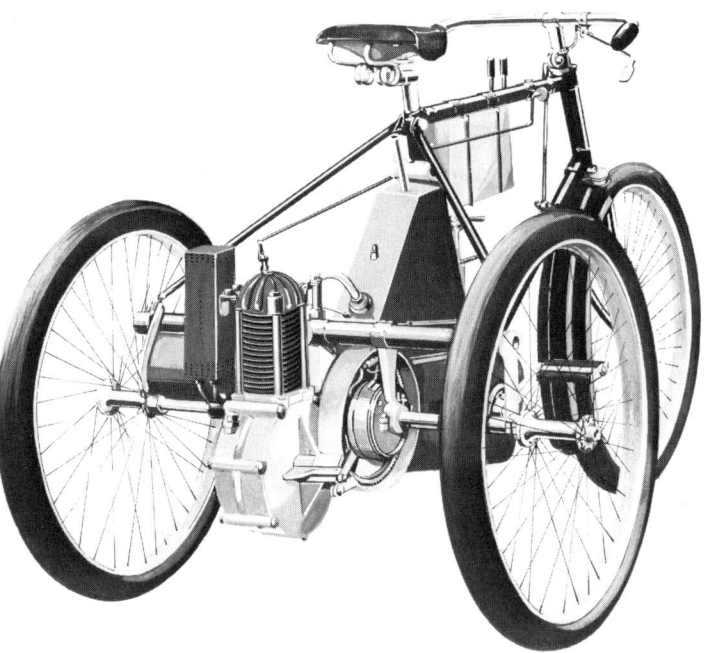

Built in August 1896, the Beeston tricycle (above) followed the De Dion design closely, except for tube ignition.
Ten years' progress is shown (below) by the machine park at the Willessey Hill Climb of the Coventry and Warwickshire Motor Cycle Club, circa 1909

in front of the steering head, driving the front wheel by belt. The engine was intended as added power rather than the sole propulsive medium – on hills the rider had to give what was euphemistically known as 'light pedal assistance'.

In many respects the Werner was cruder than most of its predecessors: 'The carburettor resembled a 2lb biscuit box full of lamp wicks, and the ignition consisted of a platinum tube kept red-hot by means of a petrol burner'.

The top-heavy layout of the Werner was less than ideal on the atrocious roads of the day, and the famous motorcycling journalist B.H. Davies ('Ixion') recalled the end of the first one he ever rode: 'It sideslipped on the grease in the Euston Road, leapt on top of its owner, pummelled him severely, and catching fire, burnt itself to scrap-iron'.

In spite of such tales, the Werner enjoyed a fair measure of popularity; Lawson bought the British rights for £4000, and his Motor Manufacturing Company (formerly the Great Horseless Carriage Company) built Werners at his Motor Mills from 1898.

But the future of the motor cycle in Britain seemed doubtful – even *The Autocar*, at that time the voice of the Lawson interests, could not arouse much enthusiasm for two-wheelers.

Reviewing the Beeston Motor Company exhibit at the 1897 Stanley Show, the journal commented: 'Recognising the uselessness of the motor bicycle for general use, the Company does not propose to continue their manufacture in large quantities'.

Fascinating and Dangerous

At the turn of the century the future of the motor bicycle was still problematical, and it generally was felt that it would never become a serious means of transport – even its keenest advocates were doubtful whether the motor cycle could ever by anything other than a toy.

Joseph Pennell, a celebrated artist-author of the day, toured France on a front-wheel drive Werner in 1900 and declared: 'But is a motor bicycle a practical touring machine? Excellent as it is for excursions, I am afraid not; . . . but is the machine practical? Is it a rival to the ordinary cycle for touring? I think not . . . the machine must be lubricated every 15 miles, and to have to stop to do so would be a bore . . . while there are no means of carrying anything but a small amount of lubricant.

But is the system right? I am afraid not for touring. I do not in this matter refer to the Werner especially, which seems to me to be the only motor bicycle at all practicable; all the others that I have seen have some fatal or absurd defect. But can a motor, of say 1 or 2 horse-power, be attached to a bicycle? Can the bicycle be made strong enough to stand the strain? And, if so, is it safe to ride, over all sorts of roads, and under all sorts of conditions? I regret to say I am afraid not . . . but, if the strength is obtained, is it safe to ride at from 12–25 miles an hour uphill and downhill, on dry and wet roads, and through traffic? Though it is most fascinating, I believe it is equally dangerous'.

As for the general public, they were convinced that the motor bicycle was a freak, although they thought that the tricycle layout – at that time being produced by upwards of fifty firms – was a practical proposition.

However, within four years the positions were reversed – the tricycle was obsolescent and the motor bicycle was the machine of the future.

Much of the credit for this change in attitudes can be given to the Continental 'clip-ons', engine units designed to clamp on to the frame of a strongly-built bicycle, driving the rear wheel by belt and pulley.

One of the earliest of these was the $1\frac{1}{3}$hp Clément, a 143cc engine capable of running at 2 000rpm. Built by one of the biggest motor manufacturers in France, the Clément was popular both on the Continent and in England where it was marketed by the C.R.Garrard Manufacturing Company of Birmingham.

Another clip-on unit, this time from Belgium, was the 211cc Minerva, built in Antwerp by Sylvain de Jong to the design of H.Luthi and E.Zurcher. The Minerva sold well, thanks to its reputation for reliability: in 1901 alone 3 000 engine units were sold, and De Jong began manufacture of complete motor cycles, although the firm's subsequent move into car production eventually meant the end of their two-wheeler output.

Third of the leading cyclemotors of the period was the Motosacoche ('toolbag engine'), built by the Dufaux brothers in Geneva, Switzerland from 1899. This was a complete unit, with fuel and oil tanks ready to bolt into any strongly-built diamond-frame pedal cycle frame to convert it into a motor bicycle.

From Britain came the ingenious Perks and Birch Motor Wheel, with a 2hp engine built into an aluminium-spoked wheel, for use between the rear forks

Minerva's first motorcycle of 1901 was rated at $1\frac{1}{4}$hp. Its 211cc engine was clipped to the down tube and drove the rear wheel through a twisted rawhide belt

The Singer Tri-Car of 1903 had its motor wheel between the front forks, but the weight of the outrigged passenger must have upset stability

of a bicycle or as the front wheel of a tricycle; the design was taken over and produced by Singer.

'Alone amongst motors of that day', recalled B.H.Davies, 'it had a reliable ignition, consisting of a low tension magneto with make and break inside the cylinder. Moreover, it had a transmission devoid of belts, for the engine drove the back wheel direct by spur gears.

That the noise of its progress would have put a worn out threshing machine to the blush was no oddity in those days. I liked this mount much. It usually got there. But it passed from my ken when its owner snapped two or three of the back wheel spokes, and had to *carry* it three miles to his home'.

The important fact about these engine attachments – and the De Dion power unit – was that they were cheap and readily available. They enabled any cycle smith to become a motor cycle manufacturer overnight, providing just the stimulus the struggling industry needed to put it on its feet.

However, by their very popularity such designs revealed the basic inability of the pedal cycle frame to absorb the extra stresses imposed by even moderate power assistance, and it became apparent that the motor cycle should be designed as a complete entity.

The first positive step in this direction was taken by Werner, who towards the end of 1901 introduced an entirely new model with the engine bolted vertically in the frame, in the position taken up by the pedal bracket on a bicycle. The pedals were moved back, emphasising their auxiliary function, and an extra cross tube beneath the fuel tank braced the frame. This design was widely copied, and before long most motor cycles had their engines fitted in the 'Werner' position. Rivals resorted to numerous dodges in order to evade the Werner patents.

One machine that did not ape the New Werner layout was the Humber, built to the design evolved by Joah Phelon, of Cleckheaton in Yorkshire, in 1900. In this the engine took the place of the front down-tube.

Humber built machines to this pattern, and Phelon received a 7s 6d royalty on each.

A pioneer motor cyclist recalled some of the features of his Humber: 'The engine formed part of the frame; it was not mounted vertically in the centre like most others. Drive was by chain, a great improvement on the rather unreliable belt drives of those days, but, since there was no gearbox, to get the necessary reduction two chains had to be used, acting through a central double pinion with one large and one small wheel. There were also pedals driving both bike and engine through chains with free wheels.

There was no kick starter: to get off one pulled over a small lever, which lifted the exhaust valve, and another which retarded the ignition. One then made a hopping start, and when in the saddle pedalled strongly. When enough speed had been reached, one dropped the exhaust lifter, and hoped that the engine would fire.

Ignition was from a trembler coil with a 4 volt battery that had to be recharged periodically. It had an automatic inlet valve, only the exhaust valve being operated by the camshaft.

Though its top speed was about 30mph, I never had any trouble with it. Traffic problems were practically negligible: the chief one was shying horses, and the driver of a horse drawn vehicle was entitled to signal to a motorist to stop if his horse showed signs of being restive.'

Like most of its contemporaries, the Humber still used the crude surface carburettor, for spray instruments were still thought too complex for the motor cycle, although they were rapidly becoming common on cars.

Reliability was not one of the stronger points of the early motor cycle, due partly to indifferent metallurgy, but perhaps mainly to the poor standards of maintenance available at repair shops. Almost any enterprising cycle agent could hang out a notice 'motors

Bucquet rode this New Werner to victory in the motor cycle section of the 1902 Paris–Vienna race

Fitted with a machine-gun, the Simms Motor Scout of 1899 was one of the earliest attempts to produce a fighting vehicle. It never reached active service

repaired' and perhaps stock a Werner or Ormonde (or any make which he could acquire on credit) without any clear idea of how to repair it when it inevitably went wrong.

Most motor cycles were driven by belt, with no clutch or gearchange, so that when the rider wished to stop, he had to stall the engine. Moreover, flat leather belts were prone to slip or stretch, and the improved V-belts that succeeded them either snapped or wore their pulleys away and became too slack. Belts lasted perhaps 2 000 miles, and punches and fasteners to rejoin them when they snapped were an indispensible part of the rider's toolkit. Rawhide 'bootlace' belts were favoured in the early days, as they could be tensioned by twisting; later, belts composed of linked segments became popular, the best being the Lincona, the Watawata and the Whittle.

Despite its faults, the belt was both smooth and silent in the transmission of power; early chain drivers, on the other hand, were harsh and liable to pull the spokes out of the rear wheel. Some of the early chain drive machines, such as the Humber, later adopted belt drive in the interests of reliability.

By 1903, the spray carburettor had become reliable enough to supplant almost completely the surface vaporiser. Tank top levers controlled the gas and air throttles, for the early carburettors were only semi-automatic, and the rider had to gauge the right fuel/air mixture to obtain the best performance.

One of the first machines to mount the engine controls on the handlebars was the 2hp Gamage of 1903, built to the designs of a leading London store; it also pioneered the twistgrip handle, with Bowden cable replacing jointed control rods.

Ignition was becoming more reliable, as the Bosch high tension magneto took over from the old coil and battery ignition. Batteries which had to be recharged between trips limited the range of the early machines, but once lightweight dynamos were perfected coil ignition was to stage a spectacular comeback (although this was many years away).

The automatic inlet valve, operated by the suction of the piston on the down-stroke, needed careful adjustment of the tension of its spring for consistent results; led by Minerva in 1902, manufacturers began fitting an extra cam to open the inlet valve mechanically.

As machines became faster and heavier, so the basic flaws in their layout became apparent. Unsprung front forks gave an uncomfortably bumpy ride, and unless specially strutted or strengthened, could snap off at the crown.

Brakes on most early machines were based on pedal bicycle practice. The stirrup front brake was completely inadequate for motor cycle performance, and its role was merely that of a 'bobby-dodger' to comply with the law – which, incidentally, in Britain decreed an overall maximum speed limit of 12mph before 1904 and 20mph thereafter, enforced by police speed traps.

Early lamps, either oil or acetylene, were usually pretty ineffectual, too, and the jarring of the machine was often enough to reduce them to their component parts before the end of a run.

Motor cycles were still comparatively expensive, prices ranging on average from £30–60, and already there was a growing opinion that they were becoming too fast (30mph or so!) and too heavy (130lb or thereabouts). Pioneer manufacturer H.O.Duncan complained: 'The horsepower of motors must obtain a standard marketable limit, which is generally supposed to vary between 1½hp and 3hp . . . racing monstrosities . . . do a considerable amount of harm to the sport, pastime and industry'.

Even so, the early motor cycles could put up some remarkable touring performances in capable hands. In 1903, for example, B.H.Davies covered 336 miles on his 2¾hp Excelsior at a total cost of three shillings!

One result of the increase in power output was that motorcyclists could now consider carrying a passenger. At first it seemed as though the tricycle would be most suitable in this respect. Pennington was one of the first to realise this, and in 1896 he constructed a three-wheeled Torpedo Autocar with a similar power unit to his moto-cycle. This had a total swept volume of 1·9 litres, its cylinders had a 62·5mm bore and an immense stroke of no less than 305mm.

The pilot sat right at the back, behind the rear axle, and the front passenger could also take a hand in the steering. Four transverse saddles for extra passengers were bestowed along the backbone of the frame. It was claimed that this sesquipedalian monstrosity could re-start on a 30 degree slope carrying 'practically four men'.

Two years later Pennington designed a more rational machine, the Olympia Tandem, which was constructed by Humber and which had a coachbuilt passenger seat mounted between the front wheels, 'nearest the accident', like another pioneer tricar, the 1896 Bollée voiturette. The rear part of the machine was on conventional motor cycle lines, with the engine outrigged behind the back wheel, a ludicrous engine position favoured by Lawson for two and three-wheelers.

Humber and other manufacturers, such as Dennis

Clipping on a wickerwork trailer turned this 1902 MMC-engined Coventry Eagle into moderately comfortable transport for two

and Royal Enfield, also built quadricycles on similar lines, but all suffered from a lack of power, and their riders had to be prepared for plenty of pedalling (and pushing!).

But this was at least preferable to the passenger's lot if the motor cyclist chose to hitch a light trailer behind his machine. On the atrocious roads of the day, the unfortunate passenger would be sprayed with exhaust fumes, oil, mud, dust and horse droppings, while the connection between cycle and trailer was unreliable — all too often it broke and the trailer careered into the ditch.

From the passenger's point of view, the attachment devised by J. Van Hooydonk, maker of the Phoenix motor cycle, was a better proposition. Van Hooydonk designed a fore-car attachment to replace the front wheel, and convert a bicycle into a two-seated tricycle (the idea was not entirely original — a similar fitment had featured on the 1898 Svea lever-driven pedal cycle from Stockholm). Tie rods clipped to the fork ends steered the front wheels, which incorporated singularly ineffectual front wheel brakes.

This Phoenix 'Trimo' attachment was widely copied, and other makers, notably Excelsior and Mills & Fulford (who had previously built trailers) were soon producing competitive designs.

One weakness of the Excelsior was the clip which attached the forecarriage to the front down tube of the cycle frame, resembling a human fist made of metal. This would gradually loosen with the vibration of the engine, so that the forecar would unexpectedly turn while the cycle kept going straight ahead. The outfit would then either overturn or ram a roadside wall.

The brief vogue enjoyed by these conversions was brought to an end by the advent of the sidecar, invented in 1902 by Mills & Fulford, who simply took one wheel off a trailer and bolted it alongside a motor cycle. Other makers soon followed their lead, and by 1903 several 'sociable attachments' were on the market. By 1911 the sidecar was firmly established.

The Mills & Fulford 'Milford' designs were always interesting, and included steerable or castoring sidecar wheels, and a one-either-side twin sidecar outfit. The growing popularity of the sidecar meant that power outputs and transmission efficiency had to be uprated to cope with the extra load; even so, the earliest sidecars were generally of wicker, to keep the weight down. Coachbuilt models began to appear after 1910.

Two ages of the tricar — the pioneering Humber Olympia Tandem of 1898, designed by Pennington, and J. Van Hooydonk's revival of the type, the 1902 Phoenix Trimo (right)

Left : the vee-twin became established quite early, as it was the easiest type of multi-cylinder engine to accommodate in a diamond cycle frame. The earliest British vee-twin models included the Birmingham-built XL-All (top) with its 90 degree engine and the narrow-angle Princeps from Northampton (centre), both dating from 1903. Three years later, the Neckarsulmer Fahrzeugwerke of Germany built this vee-twin model (bottom) with the engine inclined forward for better cooling of the cylinders
Two famous models of the early days were the 1901 Humber (above), built under Phelon patents, and the 1903 Matchless (below), with its power unit on the front down tube

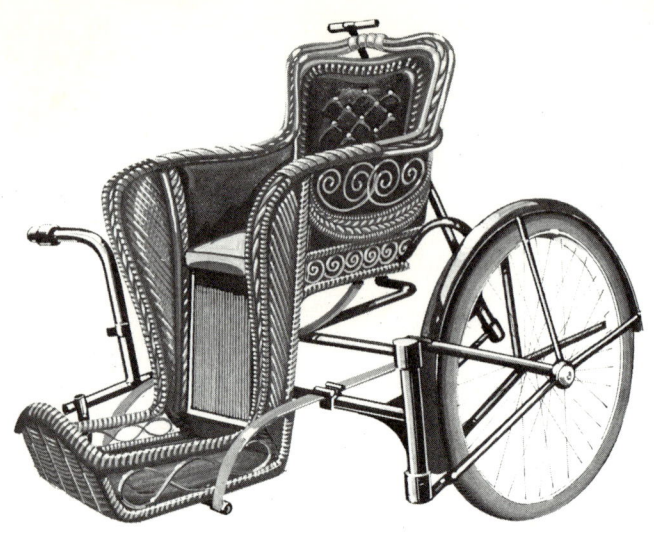

One of the very first sidecars was this rococo wickerwork Mills & Fulford Sociable Attachment of 1903. This model had a castoring wheel to aid cornering, but these earlier sidecars were 'the coldest place on earth' in windy weather

Meanwhile the purpose-built tricars were becoming more luxurious, more powerful, heavier and generally more lethargic. They had come to have the weight and price of a light car, without its social standing.

All this extra weight and complication convinced some designers that a return to simplicity was overdue and a spate of ultra-lightweight machines of varying degrees of practicality was unleashed on the market. Motosacoche at last marketed a complete machine, while the 58lb, 28 guinea KD featherweight from France was available either as a rather handsome miniature motor cycle or as a rather clumsy clip-on conversion.

A new kind of lightweight appeared in 1905, with a layout which has continually reappeared in various guises during the history of motor cycling. This was an open-framed, low-slung machine with weatherguarding – the type later to become known as the scooter. One of the earliest examples was the 1905 Brown Midget Bicar, with a steel-armoured wood frame, which was followed a couple of years later by a remarkably advanced design by W. C. Johnson of Colemans Hatch, Sussex.

In Italy in 1908 the £38 Laviosa Autocicletta was shown at Turin, with small wheels, open frame and bucket seat. This was the ancestor of all Italian scooters.

The Zenith Bicar of 1905–8 was an idiosyncratic device, with its engine, clutch and fuel tank housed in a pyramidal structure incorporating the steering head, a frame of four parallel tubes, hub centre steering and hub brakes – 'less skidding' claimed the makers.

Unorthodoxy also characterised the 1907 La Viratelle, which had a watercooled single-cylinder engine; its inlet and exhaust valves were concentric, with a positively opened and closed exhaust and automatic inlet. Other oddities tried during this period included propellor drive, a one-wheel motorcycle and an engine which ran on nitroglycerine!

Mainstream design, however, was rapidly becoming polarised, with at one end of the scale the light, often unorthodox, runabout designed for economy of upkeep, and at the other end the sporting machines for the enthusiast.

Naturally enough, the sporting riders were always looking for an increase in power and speed, and at first designers merely followed the empirical method of uprating power output by raising the swept volume of the engine. But this meant that these big singles eventually reached a size where they suffered from excessive vibration and harshness, so the industry took a second look at multi-cylinder power units, originally killed off by the clip-on boom and the New Werner type of frame, into which a vertical single fitted so neatly.

The advantages of the multi-cylinder were more even torque and increased flexibility of running. The most popular type was the vee-twin which while not quite so smooth as other multis, fitted naturally into a diamond cycle frame.

One of the first British manufacturers to fit a vee-twin was Princeps of Northampton, whose 1903 4hp model had a variable gear with handlebar control and a 'special arrangement' fitted to the inlet valves 'for regulating the tension of the springs while the engine is running so as to get the very best results out of the engine'.

In the same year the Eclipse Motor & Cycle Co, of Birmingham, built the 90 degree vee-twin XL-All. 'Two or Four horsepower at will', claimed the company, adding that in the case of a partial break down, or if the rider wanted to economise on petrol, the machine could be run on one cylinder only.

But the best known British maker of vee-twins was J. A. Prestwich, of Tottenham, London, who introduced them into his famous range of proprietory engines in 1905. A year later special pushrod ohv racing versions were introduced, notably 1 000cc and 2 700cc models.

Far smoother than the vee-twin, but difficult to house in a bicycle frame, was the flat-twin. Joseph Barter of Bristol pioneered the type in 1902, built the Fée (later Fairy) and sold the design to the Douglas Brothers of Kingswood, Bristol, in 1906. Barter's layout suffered from an excessively long engine, which gave the machine an exaggerated wheelbase and made it very liable to skid (a problem common to most early multis).

One type which did not catch on to any great extent was the vertical twin, which in its early form had most of the vibratory disadvantages of the single allied to the extra complication of the twin. Bercley of Brussels and Werner built units of this type around 1905; after a brief vogue, they disappeared from the market.

But in Bradford, Yorkshire, a quiet engineer named Alfred Angus Scott was developing an ingenious parallel twin two-stroke engine, which he first fitted to a Premier pedal cycle in 1901, driving the front wheel by a friction wheel rubbing on the tyre. By 1903 Scott had built the engine into the frame, driving the rear wheel by belt and countershaft. These early Scotts were air-cooled, but by around 1908 Scott had evolved the water-cooled engine mounted in a triangulated open frame that became the marque's hallmark. His early models were built for him by the Jowett brothers of Bradford, better known as car makers.

The ultimate in smoothness was, of course, the in-line four-cylinder. On the face of it this meant a dangerously long, and hence skid-prone wheelbase, but one way of getting round this problem was shown by Charles Binks, of Nottingham, who pioneered the four-cylinder in Britain; his 1903 model could be had with the engine set either longitudinally or transversely. But the heyday of the transverse four was many years in the future.

Late in 1904, the first examples of what was to become perhaps the most famous 'four-in-line' motor cycle were revealed to the public. Built by the Belgian armaments firm, Fabrique Nationale d'Armes de Guerre, of Herstal, Liège, the new FN model had a 363cc engine designed by Paul Kelecom, who had been responsible for the Ormonde engine, one of the best of the early single-cylinder designs. Transmission was by shaft and bevel. Soon an engine size increase to 500cc and the addition of a plate clutch and two-speed gear made this machine more practical. It enjoyed much success, and was produced for the next 20 years.

Later on, the growing popularity of the sidecar forced an inevitable return to the big-single formula,

despite the increased power output from any given engine capacity resulting from improved design. By 1914 some exceptionally large power units were being turned out – Rudge built a 750cc model with their 'Multi' belt drive, but were outdone by Excelsior, who marketed an 800cc monster – but the big-twins were equally popular for sidecar work.

The real home of the giant multi lay on the far side of the Atlantic, in the United States.

Surprisingly enough, America had been very slow to adopt the motor cycle, despite Mr Pennington's early attentions. Andrew Riker, of Brooklyn, built an electric quad in the 1890s, while Hiram Percy Maxim and the Pittsburg Motor Vehicle Co. both built De Dion-engined tricycles around the same time. Gasoline-

Shaft drive was just one of the unusual features of the 1907 La Viratelle – its water-cooled engine had just one valve opening, with concentric inlet and exhaust valves, while front suspension was distinctly odd

American pioneer. The original version of the Indian (above) was built from 1901–05; until 1909, Indian followed this leg-burning layout with the engine on the saddle tube

One of the most successful variable transmission machines was the Rudge Multi, produced from 1911 onwards (below)

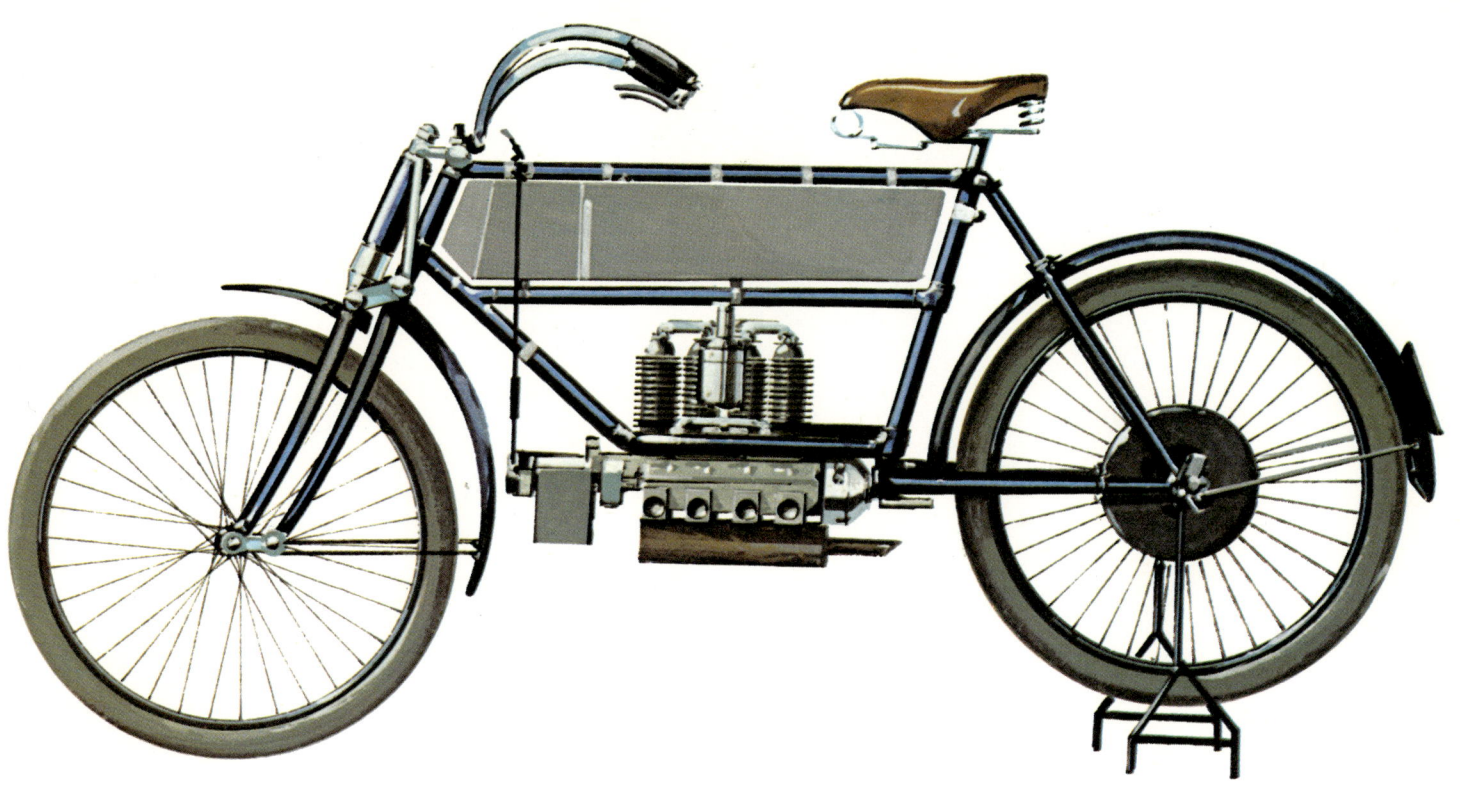

Perhaps the best known of the early four-cylinder models was the shaft-driven FN (above) built by the Belgian arsenal to the designs of Paul Kelecom. The marque retained shaft drive until Kelecom left in the 1920s, when a rapid attack of conventionality set in

This 1914 350cc Royal Enfield (below) was one of the smallest pre-First World War vee-twins. Its all-chain transmission incorporated a cush-drive rear hub. A machine of this type, ridden by F.J.Walker, took third place in the 1914 Junior TT. He crashed as he crossed the line, and was fatally injured

Two famous riders of the early days: Tom Silver (above) joined Quadrant in 1901, and was still with them in the 1920s. This is the machine he rode in the International Trophy in 1904, the year in which he also rode 6 000 miles across South Africa. Harry Martin (right) on his 3½hp Excelsior, was one of the early banked track stars. He started riding in 1901 and joined Bayliss & Thomas, makers of the Excelsior, in 1902. He later built JAP-engined machines under his own name

engined two-wheelers did not appear until after the turn of the century.

It was in 1900 that George M. Hendee, who built the Indian pedal cycles in Springfield, Massachussetts, went into partnership with Oscar Hedstrom, who designed a lightweight motor cycle with a 1¾hp engine built into the saddle tube. This went into production in 1902, when 143 were made, and the original version was produced until 1905, when it was replaced by a 2¼hp model; in 1904 handlebar twist-grips for controlling the engine were introduced.

In 1908 mechanically operated valves appeared for the first time, and power was again increased, to 3½hp. The famous Indian vee-twin models were introduced in 1905, using two 1¾hp cylinders.

The archetypal Indian appeared in 1909, with its pushrod ohv engine carried in a loop frame, and a torpedo shaped petrol tank slung from the top frame tube.

Indian were virtually unique in promoting a vigorous export policy, their British depot being in the capable hands of Billy Wells, who had formerly sold Vindec motor cycles. It was he who encouraged the entry of Indians in competitions of all kinds and the marque's consistent successes soon made it the *beau idéal* of sporting motor cyclists.

Even when well over 50, Billy Wells was still to be seen in competitive events such as the London–Edinburgh Run. The British fortunes of the Indian

Company were largely due to his efforts, and, in the early days, to the ace rider Jake de Rosier, who on October 29, 1910, performed the remarkable feat of setting up new records for all distances between 1 and 100 miles.

The other great name of the early days in the States –and still going strong today–was Harley-Davidson, founded in 1903 by William S. Harley and Arthur Davidson, who began production with a 2hp single-cylinder model with a loop frame and belt drive, which was progressively developed until 1909, when Harley built their first vee-twin, of 6hp.

Since cars were so cheap in America, from a very early date manufacturers tended to emphasise the sporting side of motor cycling. The big twin became the most distinctive and long lived American type.

A notable supplier of vee-twins to the American cycle trade was the aviation pioneer Glenn Curtiss who produced one of the more frightening racing monsters of the day by installing a V-8 engine in a frame of his own manufacture.

More sophisticated was the Cyclone, from the Twin City of St Paul, Minnesota. From 1913 until 1920 this company built overhead camshaft vee-twins, the earliest example of this form of valve operation to be produced for sale—Cyclone were in fact one of only two makers of road-going ohc vee-twins in the history of the motor cycle.

Other notable makes were the ohv Pope, from Colonel Albert Pope's motor manufacturing empire at Hartford, Connecticut, and the bright yellow Flying-Merkel, from Middletown, Ohio, which in 1913 boasted a spring frame, telescopic forks, a two-speed gearbox and a self-starter.

But however sporting the machines, American roads outside city limits were atrocious, degenerating into quagmires during the winter. This naturally limited the growth of motor cycling in that country, and led to the development of 'cars on two wheels', with unusually long wheelbases to iron out the road shocks.

The earliest of these was the Militaire, which appeared in 1911. It had car-type wooden artillery wheels and a low-slung tubular chassis; when stationary it was kept vertical by two idler wheels which were raised by a lever when the machine was under way. The driver sat in a pan seat, controlling the machine by a steering wheel. Transmission was by friction drive, giving ratios from a low of 30:1 to a high of 3:1; there was also a reverse of 10:1. The original model had an air-cooled single-cylinder engine, later supplanted by a four-cylinder power unit. The marque remained in production until 1920.

In 1913 James Scripps Booth of Detroit, produced the ultimate in two-wheeled cars, the Bi-Autogo. It had a three-seated body, a channel steel frame which passed beneath the rear axle and a massive steering head at the

front of the chassis supported sprung front forks. Idler wheels, supported the machine while at rest, as in other vehicles of this type.

The power unit of this machine was almost certainly the largest ever fitted to a two-wheeler. It was a V-8, with cylinder dimensions of 95mm by 127mm, giving a swept volume of 7202cc. There was a four-speed gearbox, in which bevel gears operated a short jackshaft carrying chain sprockets driving the rear wheel. A distinctive feature of this gigantic machine was the tubular radiator running along the side of the bonnet, which incorporated no less than 450ft of $\frac{1}{2}$in copper tubing.

But if the American motor cycle makers were losing themselves up blind alleys, the British industry had come through the sales depression of 1903–08 with flying colours.

The number of motor cyclists in Britain had grown from 29000 in 1905 to over 80000 in 1907, and the greater number of motor cycles in use meant that design imperfections were becoming more apparent and less tolerated. Moreover, the type of motor cyclist was changing – the dedicated enthusiast of the early days was being replaced by a rider who expected reliability and a reasonable performance from his mount.

Without doubt the most popular motor cycle of the 1907–9 period was the 476cc $3\frac{1}{2}$hp Triumph, made by a company established in 1885. In 1895 M. J. Schulte, a young German, came over to Coventry to demonstrate a Hildebrand & Wolfmuller motor bicycle, liked the country and stayed. He joined the Triumph Cycle company, where he soon became a director, which post he retained for over 30 years.

In 1903 Triumph began building motor cycles, at first with JAP and Fafnir power units, but in 1906 they began production of a 3hp engine of their own design. Initial models were 'uncommonly bad', and lost compression rapidly, but the company profited by their mistakes, improved the quality of their construction and soon 'enjoyed such public confidence as few firms in any industry could command'.

The essence of the Triumph's success was its simplicity of upkeep and its robust construction. Its crankshaft ran on ball bearings and the valve gear was particularly well laid out, with bellcranks interposed between the cams and the tappets. It sold at £48 – not particularly cheap for the period, but a good sporting record and proven reliability (one owner recorded 12 000 miles with a repair bill totalling only 7s 4d, for front spring parts) were powerful sales factors, and in 1908 alone the Triumph Company made a profit of £22 048.

It was the development of reliable machines on the lines of the Triumph which really established the British motor cycle industry as world leaders. Moreover, it was a vigorous industry with a remarkably high percentage of exports: in 1905, only 3 250 machines were produced, and 688 exported, but the figures rose rapidly, and by 1910, a third of the output of 10 000 machines went overseas. In 1914, annual production was running

Ariel's famous 500cc 3½hp model with a White & Poppe power unit was current from 1910 to 1925; this 1913 version has a three-speed Armstrong hub gear with free-engine clutch. In addition to the Druid front forks, the saddle pillar was sprung. The Tourist Trophy model catalogued from 1914 dispensed with the gearbox, clutch and sprung saddle in the interests of speed

1910 ASL designer Sharpe was a firm believer in pneumatic suspension. So the ASL had pneumatic springs fore and aft, giving an unusually soft ride for the period

Another early spring-frame machine was the BAT (Best After Tests) designed by S. A. Tessier. This 5/6hp model of 1913 had a fully-sprung sub-assembly carrying saddle and footboards, leading link front forks and a hand/foot starting crank

One of the most popular machines of the Edwardian era was the 3½hp Triumph, with ball-and-roller main and big end bearings and internal flywheels. This model was exceptionally reliable, and became the standard despatch riders' machine in the First World War

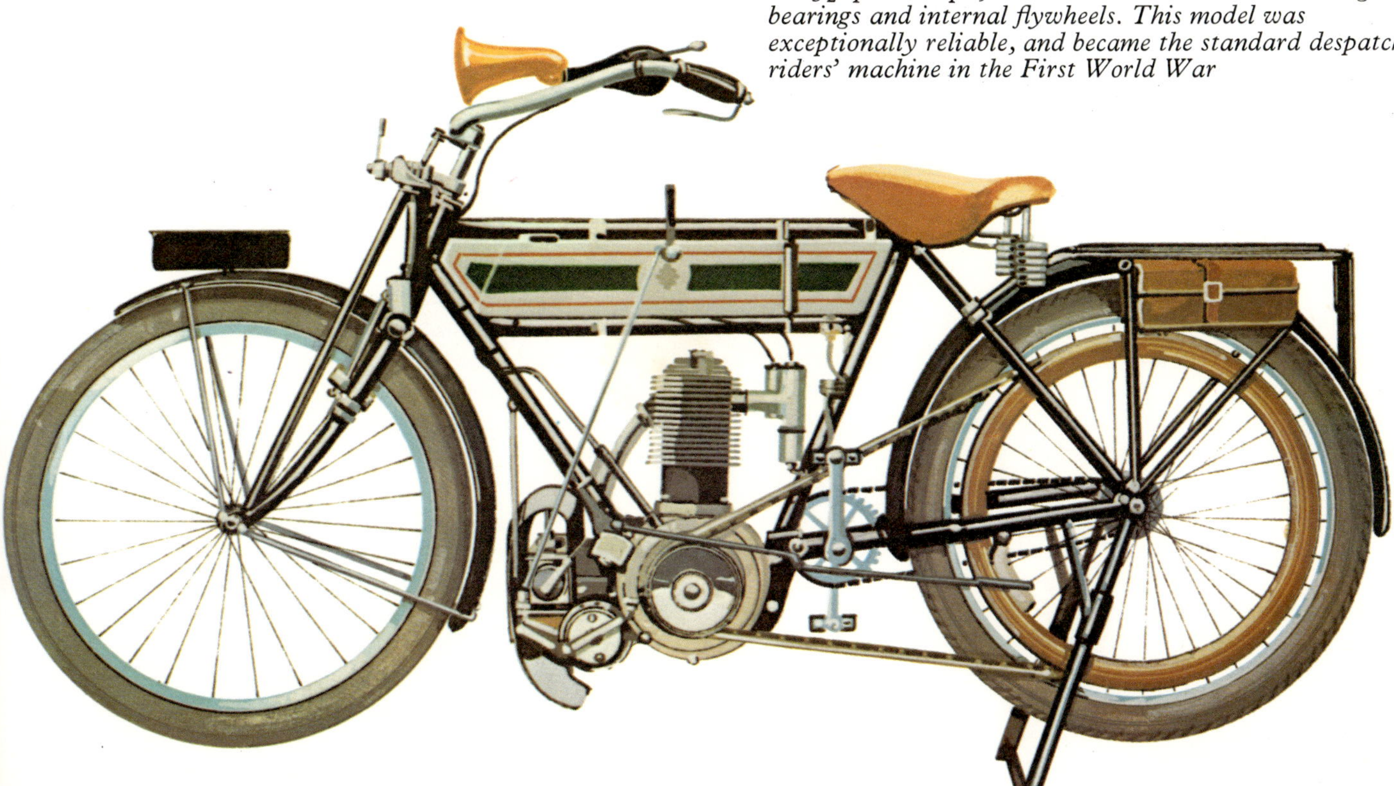

This extraordinary propellor-driven machine was designed by the wealthy French aviation pioneer Ernest Archdeacon and tested on the Achères road in 1907

at 70 000, and 20 877 were exported, with a value little short of £1 000 000.

On the Continent, however, things were very different. Although France had set the pace in the early years of the century, the number of motor cycles in use dropped noticeably between 1906 and 1909, when a low figure of 26 465 was recorded (in the same year 75 000 motor cycles were estimated to be in use in Britain). By 1912 the number of machines in use in France had risen to 37 000, but the average size of French motor cycles was smaller than their British counterparts. The most popular class was machines under 350cc, represented by Alcyon and Magnat-Debon among home products and Moto-Reve, FN and Motosacoche among imported models. Even Peugeot, one of the major manufacturers, which had made its name with big vee-twins of around 1 000cc, was concentrating on a 332cc light twin.

Typically, the French lightweight was devoid of the features demanded by the British motor cyclist, such as clutches and variable gears, for it was claimed that the low weight of the machines rendered them unnecessary. Also, the French buyer was extremely cost conscious, and often failed to see the difference between a shoddy machine at £30 and a high-grade production at nearly double that figure. Clément were almost alone in following English lines on their light twin, and it sold well.

One factor common to all the motor cycle markets was that the rider was demanding more from his machine in terms of comfort and reliability.

Vibration had been a bugbear of the early days, but the adoption of spring forks – of which the best was Druid, introduced in 1906 – had done much to alleviate this problem. The BAT ('Best After Tests') had a fully-sprung frame as early as 1903, and it was also

one of the first makes to dispense entirely with the pedalling gear, relying solely on ample engine power for its climbing abilities.

The single-speed belt transmission maintained its popularity for a surprisingly long time, due to the fact that most multi-speed gears were too flimsy, too heavy or too complex. Such pioneer efforts as the two-speed chain drive of the P & M and the epicyclic rear hub of the Roc enjoyed the confidence of the experienced rider, but for the average motor cyclist the first major breakthrough came around 1908 with the wide-spread adoption of the variable pulley.

In this, the two flanges of the driving pulley could be moved together or apart on a coarse screw thread to give a different effective diameter for the belt to run on, allowing a gear range of between roughly 4:1 and 6:1.

The disadvantage was that the pulley had to be manually adjusted for every gradient, and the belt re-tensioned. The Philipson Pulley of 1911 overcame this by springloading the pulley faces and controlling them by Bowden cable from the handlebar.

Transmission design progressed rapidly during this period. Effective though it was, the variable pulley was no more than a stop-gap measure, even in its most highly developed forms, the Zenith-Gradua and the Rudge-Multi.

In the Zenith transmission, which first appeared in 1908, a 'tram-handle' on the tank opened and closed the driving pulley, at the same time moving the rear wheel backwards or forwards, thus maintaining a constant belt tension. The Rudge drive opened and closed the rear belt pulley in conjunction with the operation of the variable pulley.

The Zenith in particular was extremely successful in hill-climbing contests, due to the ease with which it could be geared for the gradients, so it was banned from many events.

Undeterred, Zenith adopted the slogan 'Barred' and a symbolic five-barred gate as their trademark.

The first type of variable transmission to become popular was the countershaft gearbox, normally containing two ratios; it was often used with chain primary and belt final drive, and cushioning devices were being adopted on the increasing number of machines being turned out with all chain drive. Best known of these, perhaps, was the Sunbeam, introduced in 1912 as a high-quality machine for the connoisseur, which utilised the 'little oil-bath' chain casing made famous by the company's pedal cycles.

Some machines – FN, of course, Pierce-Arrow and Wilkinson – had shaft final drive, which seemed no more costly than more conventional transmissions.

Between 1910 and 1914, the epicyclic rear hub was probably the most popular form of multi-speed gearing, generally combined with some form of free-engine clutch. This meant that the machine could be pedal-started on its stand. Oddly enough, the kick-starter was only to be found on a handful of machines, such as the Scott.

The major hub designs of the period were the three-

One of the most advanced designs of 1912 was the Swan, which foreshadowed the scooters of the early 1920s with its pressed-steel open frame

Sunbeam's 1913 3½hp model had the famous 'little oil bath' chain case and a split rear axle so that punctures could be mended without removing the wheel

speed Armstrong-Triplex and Sturmey-Archer models, developed from pedal cycle practice, and not really robust enough for motor cycle work. They were soon supplanted by the improved countershaft gearbox, which by 1913 could offer up to four speeds. Some lightweights featured unit construction of engine and gearbox.

In June 1910 the Westmorland Motor Cycle Club held a non-stop run, and these three competitors tied for first place. From right to left they are W. Westwood (3½hp Triumph), H. Harrison (3½hp Bradbury) and M. Somervell, also Triumph-mounted

Other developments of the period included lower frames, sometimes with rear springing—the Sharpe-designed ASL had pneumatic suspension fore and aft—better tyres and improved lighting.

Acetylene lamps had replaced the glow worm oil lights of the pioneering days, and gave a bright, if somewhat harsh light. Experiments were being made with electric lighting, and Indian were leaders in this field, with electric lighting *and* starting in 1914.

The shape of things to come was shown by the open-framed, liberally-mudguarded Swan of 1912, but the introduction at around the same time of the clip-on Auto-Wheel, for converting a pedal cycle to power, was truly a return to first principles!

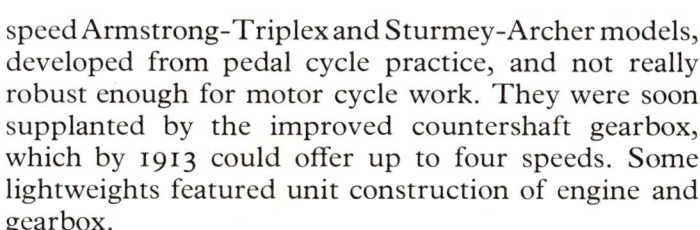

Track Tribulations

So far as the motor cycle was concerned, the famous 1900 1 000-mile trial, which really introduced motoring to Britain, was not a great success. Of five tricycles and two quads of general De Dion pattern entered, only one example of each successfully completed the trial. At the other end of the scale, the MMC tricycle finished in much the same state as the legendary Irishman's shovel, having had a new frame and wheels at Manchester and a new engine at Nottingham.

But in 1903 the Royal Automobile Club formed an Auto Cycle Club which subsequently became the Auto Cycle Union; one of the ACC's first moves was to organise a 1 000 miles trial for motor cycles. The distance was broken up into ten daily 100 mile instalments, centred on the Crystal Palace, in South London. 43 entrants started in the event, of which 20 were still in the running at the end, and proved capable, after a returning session, of achieving an average speed of 28mph in a 5 mile speed test, on the Crystal Palace cycle track.

One of the most famous early Brooklands machines was the Zenith-Gradua (below) with its infinitely-variable 'tram handle' gear. This type was popular in American speed events (right)

The organisation of the event was far from perfect, but a great deal of interest was caused, and the technical progress of the motor cycle was aided by the official discovery of a fact well-known to the riders – that the brakes then commonly used were quite inadequate. The 1903 1 000-miles trial fathered a number of similar events in the ensuing years, such as the London–Edinburgh trial of the Motor Cycling Club; the ACC developed the idea into their famous Six Days' Trial in 1905.

At first, competitors were allowed to get up the test hills anyhow – by pedalling, pushing or being towed – so long as they arrived at the route controls on time, but this era ended in 1910, as variable transmissions had become more reliable.

So far as racing was concerned, motor cycles originally ran in a separate class in the great Continental city-to-city motor races, but in 1903 an International Cup race exclusively for motor cycles was inaugurated in France. It was organised along similar lines to the Gordon Bennett motor car races: each competing nation entered three machines (and a reserve) which had to meet stringent weight limitations – the machines were to weigh no more than 108½ lb.

The 1904 International Cup race was announced only eight weeks before the event was due to take place, so the French team, as anticipated, won, and took the second and third places, too, all with Griffon machines. However, the Austrian Laurin & Klements proved unexpectedly strong challengers. The next year only three out of the 12 entrants covered the 169 mile course, and one of those was disqualified. The trouble was that manufacturers were making their racing engines (mostly big vee-twins) far too powerful for the flimsy frames – over 1 litre of engine in a 108lb all-up weight was enough to pull all the spokes out of the back wheel, as G. A. Barnes found in the eliminating trials held in the Isle of Man. Moreover, Barnes had to fretsaw leather from his saddle to get below the weight limit. This time there *was* an Austrian victory, with Wondrick (Laurin & Klement) romping in half an hour ahead of the next man, Guippon (Peugeot).

The 1905 race, held in Austria, was a walkover for the home team, riding Puchs, which came in first

This massive 2½-litre machine, built for racing ace Maurice Fournier in 1903, was intended for the French board tracks

(Nikodem) and second (Obruba). This was hardly surprising, for, despite rules closing the course to all but competing machines, the Puch riders had been assisted by sidecar outfits travelling round the course in both directions carrying spare parts and tyres.

Thus the winner finished 26 minutes ahead of Harry Collier (Britain) riding a Matchless (built by himself and his brother), who was closely followed by the German Retiene, on a Progress. Such a furore of protest arose over the Austrian tactics that the International Cup race series was abandoned.

But racing still went on, on the cycle tracks of Paris and London, where it had grown out of the use of motor cycles for pacing pedal cyclists. The British banked cycle tracks at Canning Town, Herne Hill and Crystal Palace were too gently sloped to hold really fast machines, but in Paris the Parc des Princes, the Buffalo Track and the Vélodrome d'Hiver attracted riders to develop monstrous racing bicycles and tricycles.

In 1903 Maurice Fournier built a vertical twin bicycle of around 2½ litres, weighing 360lb, for the Parc des Princes track, Paris. Even this paled into insignificance alongside the Buchet *Bête de Vitesse* tricycle, with a 4½ litre engine, which must have been quite unrideable, spending most of its time with its front wheel in the air.

A neater machine seen on the vélodromes was the 1902 Clément, the first four-cylinder racing machine. Its power unit was a compact 1 200cc V4, but the Clément proved excessively heavy, scaling 2½cwt in racing trim. Its maximum speed was around 70mph.

Incidentally, some of the French board tracks had *convex* bankings, their designers claiming that this layout was more correct than the normal concave banking.

Convinced that the Continental rules of racing,

Winner of the 1905 International Trophy was the Austrian Puch marque, which aided by a comprehensive back-up effort, repeated the victory in 1906

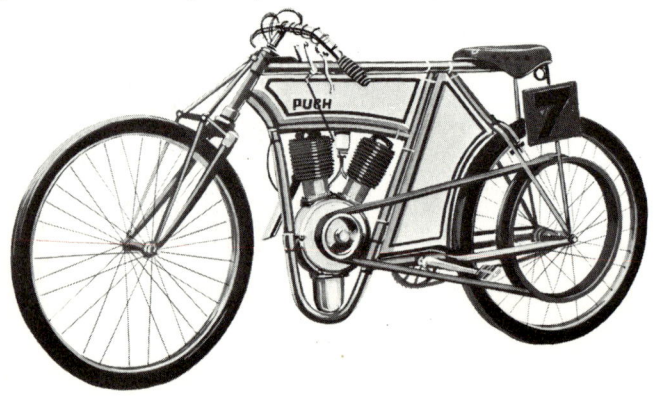

Another French track racer was the Clement V-4, with a speed capability of 70mph from a swept volume of 1 200cc

which encouraged these huge engines in scanty frames, were of little value to the development of touring motor cycles, the Auto Cycle Union decided to in-augurate a contest for machines in road trim.

Since the British Government was quite adamant about not allowing racing on the public highway (a local constable might turn a blind eye to a sprint or hillclimb meeting, but a long-distance race was something quite different), the ACU turned to the House of Keys, the autonomous government of the Isle of Man, who not only agreed to close 16 miles of road for the race, but also to subsidise the event.

In June 1907 the first Tourist Trophy race was held, open to single and twin-cylinder machines, the main restriction being on fuel consumption – singles had to cover 90 miles to the gallon, twins 75. Speeds were quite modest, though fewer than half of the 25 entrants finished the course. Charlie Collier on a single-cylinder Matchless won the race, covering the $15\frac{3}{4}$ miles in 4hr 8min 8·2sec, an average of 38·2mph, with a

H. Rembrandt Fowler won the twin-cylinder class of the first Tourist Trophy in 1907 with this vee-twin Norton, one of the first racing victories for this famous marque

petrol consumption of 94·5 miles per gallon. The twin cylinder class went to Rem Fowler's Norton, at 36·2mph and 87mpg.

Because of the amount of pedalling involved on the hills, the organisers allowed a ten minute break for riders at the halfway stage!

The 1908 event was run on similar lines, and was won by Jack Marshall on a single-cylinder Triumph $3\frac{1}{2}$hp, with Harry Reed (5hp Dot-Peugeot) winning the twin class. Marshall's overall average speed was 38·7mph, his petrol consumption over 100mpg. Some riders judged their consumption so closely that they finished with only a few drops of petrol in their tanks.

For 1909 the petrol ration was replaced by upper capacity limits of 500cc for singles and 750cc for twins. Harry Collier won on a twin Matchless at over 49mph, after an exciting duel with G. Lee Evans, in whose hands the 5hp Indian was making its TT debut. The next year, with the twin limit cut to 680cc Charlie Collier romped home at a speed of 50·7mph.

The 1911 TT was a major event in motor cycle racing for several reasons. First, engines of relatively small capacity were now performing so well that it was decided to break the TT into two separate races, the Junior, for singles of under 300cc and twins of under 340cc, and the Senior, for 500cc singles and 585cc twins. Second, the 1908 car TT 'mountain' course was to be used, with a 1 400ft climb over Snaefell and innumerable bends in its $37\frac{3}{4}$ mile lap. Then, and per-haps most important, pedalling gear was absolutely forbidden, the intention being to encourage the develop-ment of reliable variable gear systems.

Many of the more conservative manufacturers fought tooth and nail to have the ban on pedals lifted, but to no avail.

Only four of the 34 Junior machines were single-geared, most of the lightweights using Armstrong-Triplex three-speed hubs. Their speeds were phenomenal – a lap at 42mph, maximum on the flat 55mph – and the event was won by a vee-twin Humber.

Only two of the British companies competing in the Senior – Scott and P & M – had originally planned to race with variable gearing, but eventually other manu-facturers overcame their prejudices; the Collier Brothers fitted their Matchless machines with variable pulleys.

But the Indian machines came with two-speed gears as standard, and they dominated the race. At the finish, they were awarded first, second and third places (Charlie Collier came in second, 73 seconds behind the winner, O. C. Godfrey, but was disqualified for taking on petrol at an unofficial depot). And most of the single-speed Senior machines were beaten for speed by the variable-geared light weights. It was the end of the road for the ungeared racing machine.

In the 1912 Senior TT, twins were limited to 500cc. The Indian team had lost two of its best riders, Moorhouse and De Rosier, in racing accidents, and the new Scott machines looked 'very fast and held the road like postage stamps'. The race was led nearly all the way by two purple-painted Scott two-strokes

(A.A.Scott, the designer, took the colour of the tank from his sister's favourite dress) ridden by Applebee and Philipp. Near the end of the race Philipp was held up by a puncture, but Applebee covered the 187½ miles of the race at an average speed of 48·7mph. He finished six minutes ahead of Haswell's Triumph.

Since the Scott, with its unorthodox water-cooled, rotary-valved 487cc engine, was the smallest machine in the race, the four-stroke manufacturers were convinced that its engine design held some unfair advantages. So they persuaded the ACU to formulate new regulations penalising the Scott.

This did not stop Tim Wood from winning the 1913 Senior on a Scott, and nearly carrying off the 1914 event, too, before being let down by a faulty magneto. Cyril Pullin (Rudge) went into the lead and won.

In joint second place, dead-heating with Godfrey's Indian, was 'a new aspirant for TT Honours', the Sunbeam, ridden by H.R.Davies, who later became a manufacturer in his own right.

Although Britain's Brooklands motor racing track had been opened in 1907, motor cycle racing had not featured in its first season. In fact, the first two-wheeler race at Brooklands was a private match contested on February 25, 1908, between W.G.McMinnie's TT Triumph and O.L.Bickford's Vindec, which was won by the former. This was so successful that in April a full-scale motor cycle race at the Easter Monday car race meeting attracted 24 entrants, with engines ranging from 331 to almost 1 000cc. Not unexpectedly, the biggest, most powerful machine won, a single-speed belt-drive 986cc vee-twin NLG-Peugeot, ridden by W.E.Cook. This machine, the first ever built by its manufacturers, North London Garages, was extensively lightened and weighed only 118lb all-up; holes were drilled in clips and nuts to save weight, and the cooling fins of the engine were filed off where possible and pierced otherwise. The NLG finished over half a mile ahead in a 5½ mile race, at a speed of 63mph; its maximum speed was in the region of 76mph, yet it was quite devoid of springing and its 26 × 2in beaded-edge tyres were little larger than those on pedal cycles.

This combination of rider and machine proved almost unbeatable during the track's early days.

The second event was organised a month later, on a handicap basis, which proved much fairer, and resulted in a much closer finish. Motor cycle races became regular fixtures at Brooklands, and were very largely responsible for the improvement in performance of British motor cycles.

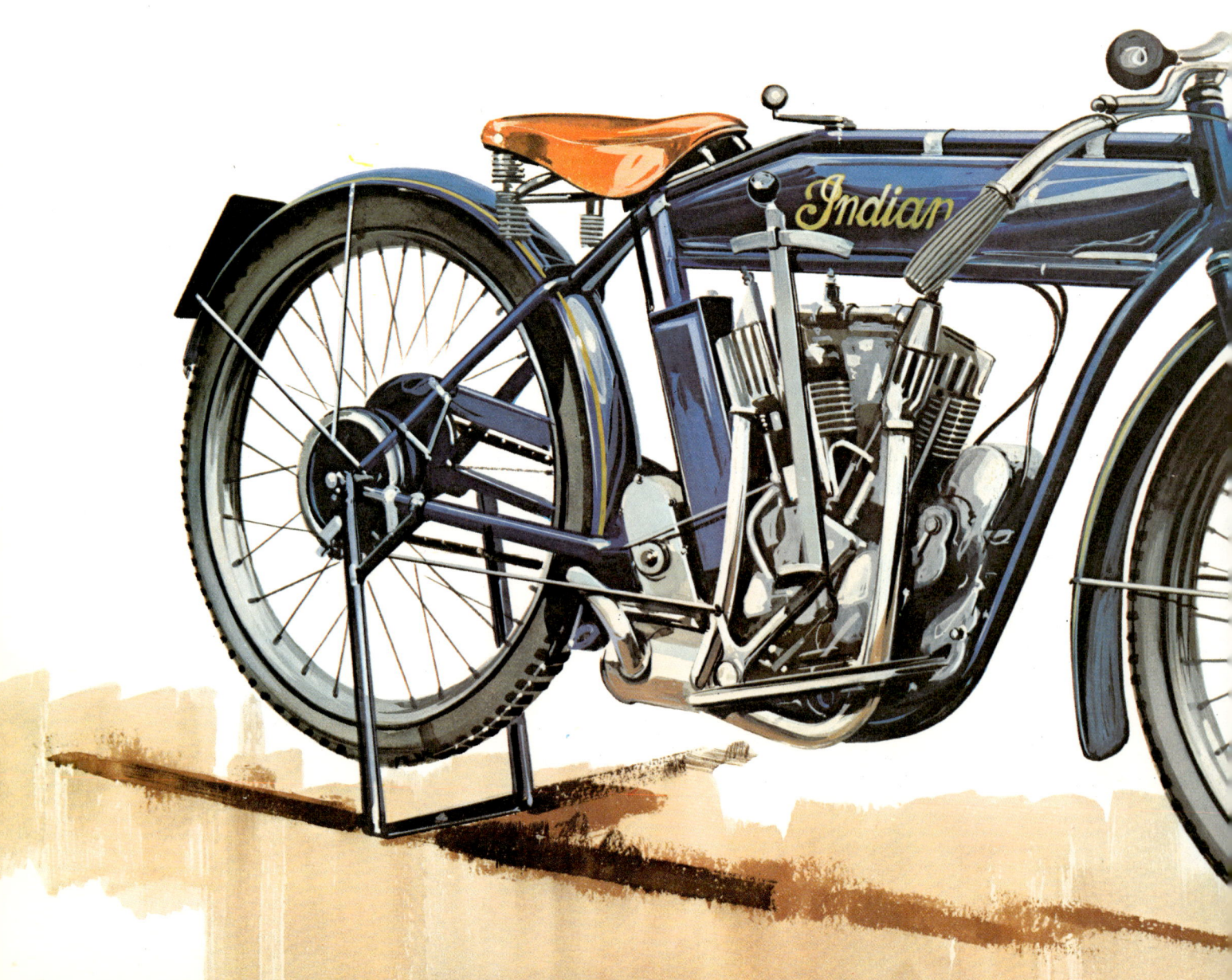

Tim Wood (above) won the 1913 Tourist Trophy on this parallel-twin two-stroke Scott after a ding-dong Scott–Indian–Rudge battle for first place that lasted throughout the race

The 1911 TT was won by a 994cc Indian vee-twin (left) ridden by O.C. Godfrey. This model developed around 25bhp at 2 500 rpm, weighed less than 200lb and was capable of up to 90mph. Contributing to its racing success was a simple two-speed dog-and-chain transmission allied to a free-engine clutch. The throttle, unusually, was operated by the left-hand, and was a twist grip, a layout pioneered by Indian. Incidentally, the German Pfalz triplane of the 1914–18 war had a handlebar twistgrip throttle before this arrangement became common on motor cycles

Gala Day of the Associated Clubs at Brooklands, July 1910: the start of the Auto-Cycle Union short distance handicap

One of the most famous motor cycle events to be held at the track was a three race challenge match run off in 1911 between Jake de Rosier, 'the American crack', on an Indian, and Charlie Collier, victor of the 1907 Tourist Trophy on a single-cylinder 3½hp Matchless. The scene at Brooklands as the two little coteries prepared for the fray was unforgettable. The two Collier brothers, Harry and Charlie, and the faithful Bertie Colver, their right-hand man, had their machine tuned to a nicety, while the American pit crew cosseted de Rosier's vermilion vee-twin as though it were a living thing.

'They left nothing to chance', recalled Brooklands signwriter Bert Dicker, an eyewitness of the great match, over half a century later. "I was told that they brought their own petrol over from America".

'Schebler carburettor he had on, I remember', added his brother Bob, later a racing motorcyclist himself.

The two contestants each won a race, then Jake de Rosier came in first in the deciding event. But it was a close-run thing.

'There was only a wheel's distance between them', concluded Bert Dicker.

British pride was to some extent assuaged later in the year, when Charlie Collier smashed all the records set on American tracks. At Brooklands he covered a flying mile at the then–phenomenal speed of 91·37mph.

Those early track bikes ran in such an extreme state of tune that they would only hold their tune during the race itself–it was not possible to ride the machine to and from the venue.

Shortly before his death in the late 1960s, Bert Dicker recalled those days before sophisticated works back-up: 'I was going from Weybridge to Byfleet, and I remember seeing three motorcyclists in tight leggings and black leather breeches walking from the track pushing three nice little bikes–they were Charlie Collier, Harry Collier and Bertie Colver, representing Matchless. To see those three walking home with their bikes . . . they used to have little leather bags with all the

tools in and one or two magnetos, and other spare things strapped to their bikes. Old Harry Martin was another one who used to do that and Vic Horsman . . . in the early days, they didn't ride them on the road'.

Bob Dicker remembered a more macabre detail of pre-First World War Brooklands: 'Arthur Moorhouse was attempting to break long-distance records on an Indian motor cycle in 1912. His exhaust system came loose, and one of his mechanics signalled to him. He looked round, steered off and hit a telegraph pole with his head. Poor Arthur! I rushed up–there was his helmet with half his head inside–it was terrible! They buried the bike near where he came off, down the Railway Straight. And for all I know, it's still there'.

This Matchless vee-twin won the 1910 Senior Tourist Trophy, ridden by Charlie Collier at an average speed of 50·7mph. His brother Harry was second on a sister machine

Motoring for the Millions?

The coming of the cyclecar was called 'the new motoring', although it was really nothing of the kind. The cyclecar, a light three or four-wheeler powered by a motor cycle engine, was the lineal development of the old tricar.

What was perhaps the first cyclecar was produced in 1906 by Robinet of Nantes, Loire-Inférieure, France. It was a curious 19hp four-wheeler of spindly construction with tandem seating. The driver sat at the rear, and the vehicle was powered by a vee-twin Deckert engine. It was only on the market a year.

In England in 1908 John Weller produced a two-seated passenger version of his Auto-Carrier tradesman's box tricycle, with tiller steering and rear-mounted 5/6hp engine; priced at under £100, it sold well until 1914.

But the archetypal cyclecar did not appear until 1910, the brainchild of a red-bearded Frenchman named Bourbeau and his partner Devaux, of Paris; known as the Bédélia, it was tandem seated, like the Robinet, and also featured rear seat steering (the front axle pivoted in the centre, like a horse drawn four-wheeler). It was belt-driven. Power was either by a hefty single-cylinder engine or else a thumping vee-twin, which was capable of propelling the Bédélia at velocities far in excess of the capabilities of its exiguous steering and brakes. The petrol tank, which not infrequently leaked, was immediately above the engine.

Thomson Brothers of Bilston, Staffordshire, built this three-wheeled cyclecar in the 1920s; now the company makes tanker lorries

Most successful of the sporting cyclecars was the Morgan:
the Grand Prix model (above) celebrated the company's
success in the 1913 Cyclecar Grand Prix. Air ace Albert
Ball owned one of these machines. The Aero (below)
of the 1920s carried on the tradition

But this motorised accident looking for somewhere to happen was adapted as an ambulance during the First World War, with a stretcher slung above the bonnet and front seat; only the healthiest of casualties can have survived the trip.

In 1910 H. F. S. Morgan, son of the Rev H. G. Morgan, Prebendary of Stoke Lacy, near Malvern, Worcestershire, began production of an ingenious three-wheeler based on a 1909 prototype constructed in the workshops of Malvern College and using the vee-twin Peugeot engine from a crashed motor cycle. The tubular backbone of the frame also housed the propellor shaft, and a bevel box at the rear drove the rear wheels via chains (there were two ratios, engaged by dog clutches). Front suspension was independent, by sliding pillars. As developed, the Morgan became a fast sporting machine; the marque won a moral victory in the 1913 Cyclecar Grand Prix at Amiens.

Equally as sporting was the four-wheeled GN, ancestor of the Frazer Nash car, and the Morgan's closest rival, later advertised as 'The Doom of the Sidecar'.

The cyclecar craze caught on quickly in Britain and France, although attempts to popularise it in America were dismal failures. By 1912, the peak year of the 'new motoring', cyclecar factories were springing up like mushrooms – and generally vanishing as quickly –

and there was a brief vogue for converting antique tricars into more or less lethal cyclecars.

The natural tendency was for the cyclecar to develop into a 'large car in miniature' like those built by Singer, GWK, Bugatti and Peugeot – the cruder type of cyclecar had virtually – but temporarily – vanished by 1915.

The post-World War One demand for cheap transport proved an inestimable boon as far as the cyclecar industry was concerned, for the car buying public was neither experienced nor critical enough to pass up even the most crude designs, such as the AV and the Gibbons, which combined the less desirable features of pre-war designs such as centre-pivot steering, wood-plank chassis, and wire-and-bobbin steering in conjunction with more powerful engines, giving an even greater potential for mischief.

The Gibbons, especially, had the air of being constructed from old teachests, and had its engine bolted to the offside of the body in the open air, where it could be cooled by the wind and the rain.

In complete contrast was the Scott Sociable, developed by Alfred Scott after he had sold his interest in the motor cycle bearing his name. True, it carried its engine on the offside, but it was covered in. The power unit, not unexpectedly, was a vertical twin two-stroke of 578cc, which drove the offside rear wheel through a three-speed constant mesh gearbox and shaft

This quaint little delivery van was built in 1913 by Girling in an attempt to gain some of the market sector held by Autocarrier

39

Alfred Scott's unorthodox Sociable was an attempt to give the sidecar formula small car comfort, but its strange appearance proved its downfall

and bevel transmission. The three wheels were laid out in the same manner as on a sidecar outfit, but were detachable and interchangeable. The chassis was built up on a system of triangulated tubes, only four different lengths being used throughout the machine, and there were only three greasing points on the chassis. Body construction was equally unorthodox, with panelling in waterproof fibre reinforced by ash strips.

While the Scott Sociable was an extremely practical design, sales were poor due to its unconventional appearance – it looked as if a fourth wheel had fallen off.

The bottom soon dropped out of the cyclecar market. The cruder models were obviously doomed from the start, but the more refined three-wheelers like the TB and the Castle Three, which followed 'real' car practice more closely, failed because their very refinement spelt added weight and cost; and they could not compete as far as price was concerned with the Austin Seven. Even in France, where customers were more tolerant of crude or eccentric design, cyclecars still tended to grow up into light cars.

Only the Morgan continued to enjoy both commercial and competitive success, and was built under licence in France as the Darmont, and later as the Sandford. The most famous Morgan of the 1920s was the Aero introduced at the 1919 Motor Cycle exhibition, and developed from the pre-war 'Grand Prix' model. With its long-tailed body, twin aero windscreens and 1100cc vee-twin power unit, the Aero

Morgan was the most desirable sporting cyclecar available, and its price was considerably less than other three-wheelers of lower performance.

In 1922 a real show-stopper was built by Morgan in the form of an Aero with a nickel-plated brass body and a boa-constrictor bulb horn.

Then, in 1927 came the even more outstanding 'M' type Super Sports Morgan with lowered chassis and streamlined coachwork. Racing versions of this model were the fastest three-wheelers in the world, and held 84 per cent of the world's records in all classes from 350–1100cc by 1929.

The only other make to challenge Morgan at all seriously was the front-wheel-drive BSA of 1929, but the Morgan outlasted it by almost 20 years.

Even more uncouth was the Grice three-wheeler of the mid-1920s, built by the 'G' of GWK

War and Peace

When war broke out in August 1914, there was a tremendous demand for motor cycle despatch riders for immediate service with the first seven divisions of the British Expeditionary Force. Initially these men were recruited through *The Motor Cycle*; the part they played was most important, for wireless communication was still in its infancy. The War Office at first bought large quantities of secondhand motor cycles, advertising for experienced riders, but the numbers of makes in use posed problems when it came to maintenance in the field.

Consequently the Army standardised on two-speed 2¾hp Douglas and three-speed 4hp belt-driven Triumph Model H machines, while the Royal Flying Corps used 3½hp P & M motor cycles.

Sir John French, Commander-in-Chief of the British Expeditionary Force, wrote of the despatch riders: 'Carrying despatches and messages at all hours of the day and night in every kind of weather, and often traversing bad roads blocked with transport, they have been conspicuously successful in maintaining an extraordinary degree of efficiency in the service of communications . . . no amount of difficulty or danger has ever checked their energy and ardour'.

More spectacular, if less effective, was the Motor Cycle Machine Gun Corps, which used armoured sidecars to carry Vickers machine guns and ammunition. Clyno and Royal Enfield vee-twin outfits were favoured by the MMGC, which also used Matchless and Scott machines. Some of the Clyno outfits—about 1 500—found their way to Russia. Later the MMGC became the Heavy Machine Gun Corps, using armoured cars.

The motor cycle had shown itself capable of taking over the role traditionally taken by the cavalry, a development the generals were not capable of appreciating.

When the war was over, the climate was peculiarly favourable to sales of new motor cycles. Thousands of returning servicemen had their first taste of powered transport during the war, and wanted a motor vehicle of their own—and obviously the motor cycle was within the reach of a wider section of the population than the motor car.

Aero engine developments during the war had solved many of the technical problems of the air-cooled engine, and the number of trained mechanics had been vastly augmented by the needs of the motorised wing of the military.

Unfortunately, the motor cycle industry, sensing this sellers' market, rushed into production with new and untried designs, with inadequate costing of the parts and labour, and many of the manufacturers who had attempted to break into the market with all-new models found their sales rapidly falling away.

The case of the Sopwith Aviation Company was typical. It took over production of the flat-twin ABC, originally designed in 1913 by that wayward genius,

The Vickers-Clyno motor machine gun outfit was one of the First World War's more unorthodox weapons. Scott, Royal Enfield and Zenith also built machine gun carriers

Granville Bradshaw, whose engines never seemed to get the development they deserved. Fully sprung fore and aft, with steel cylinders, aluminium pistons and unit construction of the engine and four-speed gearbox, the ABC attracted thousands of orders.

Production difficulties caused the price to rocket upwards, while the ohv engine was found to shed its pushrods if over-revved. Only a relative handful of ABCs had been built when the cash ran out; had it been properly developed, it would have been a world-beater.

It was a lack of finance, too, that doomed one of the most remarkable post-war motor cycles, the Superb Four. Built in Anerley, South London, it was designed by W. F. Hooper, whose previous experience had been in aero engine work.

The Superb Four engine was a remarkable piece of work – 'the finest motor cycle engine ever produced' reported *Motor Cycling*. It had an air-cooled 1000cc four-cylinder unit with a single overhead camshaft.

Extensive use was made of cast aluminium, and there was a positive oil feed to all the working parts (most contemporary machines still required the rider to pump oil to the bearings every few miles).

Unfortunately the Superb Four Motor Company was grossly under-capitalised, and, after building only a handful of machines in 1921–22, they ceased production, and Hooper turned his attention to lightweight machines.

Manufacturers who built less precocious motor cycles, however, rode a wave of success. During the boom of 1920–21 prices temporarily rose to four times the pre-war level – even so English production in each of those years was 75 000, 5 000 more than the 1914 total, and it continued to rise steadily.

In its overall specification, the post war motor cycle was immeasurably improved. Quite apart from the improvement in cylinder cooling, the old system of lubrication, which relied on the rider replenishing the crankcase supply by a hand pump mounted on the

petrol tank, was being replaced by mechanically-operated dry sump systems.

Robust countershaft gearboxes were also a standard item of equipment, except on the lightweight machines, which were often the products of one-man firms using proprietory engines, and retained belt drive in a last-ditch stand against progress. Paradoxically their engines were usually two-strokes of less than 250cc, a type that was only just coming into its own.

The mid-1920s was a fruitful period in engine design, and there was a wide variety of power units on the market. Velocette (above) popularised the overhead camshaft on this 1925 350cc machine, while Packman & Poppe (far left) built the neat P & P Silent Three with a 350cc Barr & Stroud sleeve-valve engine. Scott's parallel-twin two-stroke theme was ably continued by the 1926 Flying Squirrel (below left), while Dunelt's 500cc single two-stroke (below) had supercharging provided by its 'top hat' piston

Granville Bradshaw's 398 cc ABC flat-twin was, so the legend goes, designed in his bath on Armistice Night to enable the Sopwith Aviation Company to adapt to peacetime production

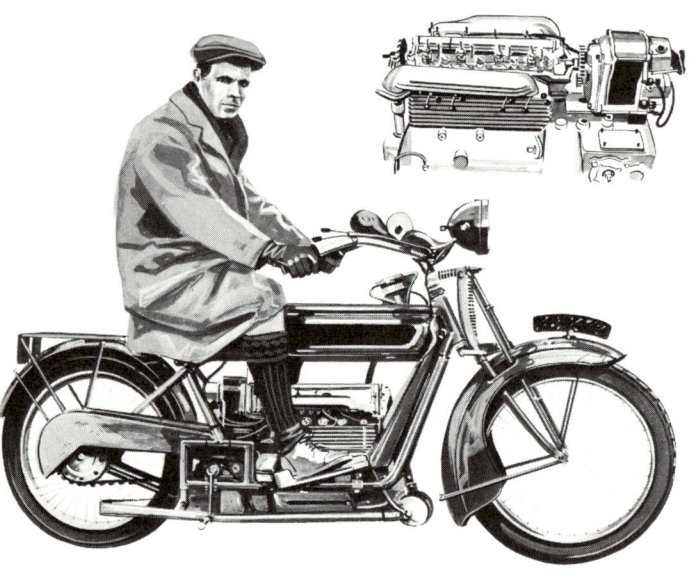

Press comments may have dubbed the Superb Four (above) 'the finest motor cycle ever produced', thanks to its overhead camshaft in-line alloy block four-cylinder engine, but most post-war buyers preferred conventional machines like the 1920 James 5/6 hp model 9 three-speed twin (below)

Soon, in the quest for power, overhead valves began to be used, especially on the proprietory Blackburne and JAP engines. Improved cylinder head design, more sporting valve timing and the replacement of cast-iron pistons by aluminium all played their part in increasing performance.

Sales rose, in Britain at least, by leaps and bounds. In 1923, over 100 000 machines left the factories, and the figures continued to rise until 1927, when 163 024 motor cycles were made. From then on, as the slump tightened its grip, output fell rapidly; it was not to pass the 1927 level until 1949.

The variety of engine types used during the 1920s was quite considerable. At the 1920 Olympia Show there were 96 exhibitors; 61 of them showed four-stroke engined machines and 48 showed two-strokes. Surprisingly, the vee-twin was the most popular configuration – 50 models featured such a power unit. Next came the single-cylinder four-stroke; there were 48 of these, followed closely by 46 single-cylinder two-strokes. A poor fourth came flat-twins (11), with the Scott the sole representative of the two-cylinder two-stroke *and* the water-cooled motor cycle.

Alfred Scott had sold his interest in the firm in 1919 for £50 000 in order to concentrate on the production of the unorthodox three-wheeler already mentioned, which had been developed from an abortive machine gun carrier of 1915. The design of the Scott motor cycle was changed only in minor details. The Scott might be termed the Bugatti of motor cycles – its excellence of finish, smooth running and outstanding performance 'established a genuine cult of an almost religious character'. But the company suffered from under-capitalisation.

In 1926 they introduced a new model, the Flying Squirrel, in 498 cc and 596 cc forms, which was initially produced alongside the old open-framed 486 cc Squirrel

and 496cc Super Squirrel models. Of more conventional appearance than its predecessor, the Flying Squirrel was a worthy upholder of the Scott tradition.

The other notable two-stroke design of the 1920s was the Dunelt, made in 250 and 500cc forms, which had a double-diameter 'top hat' piston, giving a degree of forced induction, which the company glorified as 'supercharging'.

On the four-stroke front, perhaps the most significant innovations were made by Harry Ricardo, whose connection with the motor cycle had begun in 1902 at Rugby School, when he had fitted his pedal cycle with a single-acting Uniflow steam engine with twin vertical cylinders and a coal-fired fire-tube boiler. It was, he recalled, an 'absurd machine', and capable of running no more than 200 yards at a time.

Then, at Cambridge, he built a 900cc petrol cycle with many distinctive design features. It proved itself capable of achieving nearly 160mpg at a speed of 25mph, and opened the door to Ricardo's subsequent career in internal combustion engine design.

During the First World War Ricardo was closely concerned with the design and development of tanks. After the Armistice he became increasingly concerned with fuel technology, and the associated problem of increasing engine compression ratios for greater power and efficiency. One of his projects was the design of a cylinder head for side-valve engines that would enable them to develop a comparable output to the overhead valve unit. This he successfully achieved, but took the project a stage further in designing an overhead valve conversion for the 500cc Triumph which his assistant, Franek Halford, raced at Brooklands.

The new cylinder head, which had four valves operated by the existing tappet mechanism was an immediate success when combined with Ricardo's new racing fuel, raising the machine's output to around 25bhp, approximately the same as a contemporary 1·5 litre family car engine.

Halford began winning races with ease, and much of the credit went to the new fuel, which was eventually banned at Brooklands, because it supposedly conferred too much benefit on the user. Triumph, however, knew better, and they asked Ricardo to adapt his design for commercial use on road-going bikes.

The result was the Triumph-Ricardo, with a four-valve cylinder head engine. It combined high running speed with high power, and was produced with much commercial success over a period of years.

The road-holding qualities of the machine were reputed to have been treacherous, but this was not Ricardo's design problem. He had shown how to get the most from a power unit of comparatively modest dimensions; it was a bold piece of original research which was to prove of immense value in the development of the motor cycle.

At around the same time that Ricardo was developing the overhead valve Triumph, J.A.Prestwich & Company were popularising the overhead camshaft – pioneered by the short-lived Superb Four – in Britain. Experimental 500cc and 350cc models with this feature ran in the 1922 TT Races. Soon, other makers turned to the overhead cam in their search for power.

Velocette, previously best known for lightweight machines, featured an ohc engine in their 350cc range for 1925, and in 1926 they won the Junior TT with a motor cycle of this type. Then, in 1928, they introduced the positive stop foot gear change – kick up for an upchange, down to change down – which over the next decade or so was to completely supplant the old tank-mounted lever.

Again they won the TT and in honour of their victory produced the KTT, the first 'over-the-counter' racer offered to the public. The ohc design proved capable of almost infinite development, and the KTT, in much improved Mk VIII form, was still going strong in the 1950s.

Norton introduced an overhead camshaft machine, the CS1, in 1927, while Calthorpe and Humber were other makers listing ohc sports models.

Two more off-beat engine types made their mark in the early 1920s. The first to appear was another design by Granville Bradshaw, in which the cylinder was immersed in the crankcase up to its shoulders. The theory was that the oil splashing around inside the crankcase would keep the engine cool; the unit's nickname 'oil-boiler' seems to dispute this idea, but the engine was quite widely used in motor cycles and light cars. However, air-cooling had by now reached the pitch where artificial aids to coolness were unnecessary, and the vogue for the Bradshaw engine was quickly over.

And the other power unit was the product of Barr & Stroud, 'an old established firm of skilled engineers, makers of range finders fire control gear, submarine periscopes and other naval, military and scientific instruments of great precision'. They produced, late in 1920, a sleeve valve power unit based on the Burt-McCollum single-sleeve design. This did away with the conventional valve mechanism; instead, the piston rose and fell in a sleeve, which itself moved up and down in the cylinder. As it moved, the sleeve twisted to and fro, so that slots cut in it coincided with the inlet and exhaust ports at the appropriate moment.

They claimed it was 'lighter, more efficient, more silent and more economical then any other motor cycle engine of the same dimensions'. But sleeve valve tecnology was still in its infancy, and the piston, the sleeve and the cylinder all expanded at different rates when hot, resulting in some interesting metal puzzles for the repair man!

The Bradshaw and the Barr & Stroud at least went into production, which is more than can be said of the ingenious Redrup engine, which promised absolute freedom from vibration. Appearing in 1919, it was a 309cc three-cylinder radial engine, with the cylinders at 120 degrees.

Only a few were made, but two of these units were mounted together in a single frame to produce what must have been the world's first six-cylinder motorbike.

A similar unit, the 870cc three-cylinder radial Eta,

'Unorthodox' sums up the five-cylinder Megola of 1921–25, which combined advanced design features with an absence of transmission and clutch

seemed equally set for success with a fully-sprung, cradle frame and shaft drive, but it too fell by the wayside.

And then there was the curious Megola, which must surely rank as the oddest motor cycle ever to reach production status. Designed by Fritz Cockerell, and built in Munich, the Megola had a 640cc five-cylinder rotary engine inside the front wheel, and a fully sprung, pressed-steel frame with ample weather-guarding and a comfortable seat complete with padded backrest.

But Cockerell, who was also responsible for some of the best engineered conventional German machines of the 1920s, seems to have been of the opinion that making the rider too comfortable might result in a race of effeminate motor cyclists, so he completely contradicted the advanced design of the Megola by omitting to equip it with either clutch or gearbox.

So the unfortunate rider had to push-start the machine, and switch off at every traffic hold up. Heaven help him if the ignition switch ever failed to stop the engine, for the Megola went like a scalded cat – it gained an impressive competition record.

Over 2 000 of these strange machines were built in the period 1921–25. In fact, the demand for Megolas was just one facet of the amazing revival of the German motor cycle industry in the early 1920s. Although that country had suffered such a crushing defeat, and her

economy was in ruins, the motor cycle industry flourished as never before, with a truly phenomenal number of individual firms building machines to meet the demand.

Many of these companies, of course, were one man and a dog concerns, living from hand to mouth and cobbling up unremarkable machines from bought-out components, but there were a great many remarkable and original designs among the dross.

One of the earliest German companies to commence production after the war was Ardie of Nuremburg, initially with a 350cc single-cylinder two-stroke. Then in 1925 a range of JAP-engined models of 250 to 1 000cc capacity was introduced; duralumin frames were used in the late 1920s, a feature shared by Ernst Neumann-Neander's unorthodox Neander machines from Cologne.

DKW (Der Kleine Wunder: the little wonder) did much pioneer work in two-stroke development. At first they revived the veteran Bichrone layout of a separate pumping cylinder that could deliver the fuel with some degree of supercharging, but their adoption in 1929 of

French machines of the 1920s varied in design from the basic, like the Gnôme et Rhône of the mid-1920s (top) to the magnificent ohc Koehler-Escoffier vee-twin (above). But sporting machines sold poorly in France, and in 1929 Koehler-Escoffier were taken over by Monet-Goyon, ending their days producing utilitarian two-strokes American buyers of the 1920s, however, liked their machines big, and the ACE, built by Indian, was no exception, with its 1229cc four-cylinder engine

Epoch-making two-stroke—the 1929 DKW two-stroke, which pioneered the flat top piston layout. It was built in Zschopau-in-Sachsen, Germany

Dr Schneurle's loop-scavenge system, in which the old deflector-topped piston was replaced by a flat-topped piston and better port layout, was a major landmark.

Equally significant was the introduction of the 500cc transverse-twin shaft drive BMW in 1923. This successful design showed the unfulfilled potential of the ABC layout.

The French motor cyclist, on the other hand, was hardly concerned with technical excellence—all he wanted was basic transport, and the manufacturers rose (or fell) to meet his demands with an unsightly rash of sub-utility lightweights in which every refinement was thrown overboard in the interests of economy and low selling price.

The Cyclotracteur and the Micromoteur were typical examples of a type which has persisted in France right up to the present day, comprising a small single-cylinder unit mounted in front of the steering head and driving the front tyre by friction roller. Other makes had the motor on the luggage grid, clipped to the frame or even rolling along in a little trailer behind the cycle.

Another French lightweight of the mid-1920s was the Automoto two-stroke. The Automoto company subsequently passed into the Peugeot cycle group

The only French maker to achieve serious production with a conventional motor cycle in the early 1920s was Blériot, better known for their flying machines. The Blériot range consisted of two models, both vertical twins—a type then unknown in England—of 500cc and 750cc.

Both models had a rusticity of appearance which hardly appealed to the English motor cyclist. More to their taste was the limited output Koehler-Escoffier from Lyons, a quality machine with a high-efficiency vee-twin engine. This company's 1922 Sport had a 500cc ohv engine capable of running at 4000rpm, and an early type of telescopic front fork. But their most famous model was the mighty 1000cc, which had twin overhead camshafts and which was almost certainly the most powerful French motor cycle ever built, as well as Europe's only production ohc vee-twin.

La Viratelle were still in production—just—with a 350cc water-cooled parallel twin and Gnôme at Rhône were building ABCs under licence, but the general picture in France was one of low power output and mediocre design.

But even this depressing state of affairs was preferable to the design doldrums on the far side of the Herring Pond, where the motor cycle market in the United States was virtually moribund. The advent of the cheap mass-produced car—a brand new post-Armistice Ford cost less than $600 (approximately £125)—had captured that section of the market that required merely low-cost transportation. And the major slump in the motor industry in late 1920 when Ford prices were slashed to $440 to counter stagnant sales smashed another nail into the two-wheeler's coffin.

There was still a limited market for the big in-line four of around 1 litre, like the Henderson and its first cousin the Ace, later produced under the Indian banner. One of the last American lightweights, the 270cc worm-drive Cleveland, was supplanted in the mid-1920s by big fours. Generally the motor cycle was sold purely on its sporting merits.

The recession of the early 1920s reduced the American motor cycle industry to a handful of companies which were large enough to weather the storm. Dominating the scene were Indian and Harley-Davidson, with Excelsior (sold in England as the Big-X) still in the running but a long way down the field.

While the rest of the world progressed, the design of the American motor cycle became crystallised almost to the point of cliché.

One major factor in the survival of Indian and Harley-Davidson was that both makes were extremely popular as mounts for speed-cops.

So, if you really wanted to see the widest spectrum of motor cycles, England was the place to be. Although the trend was towards the overhead valve machine, for passenger work the good old slogging sidevalve still held its own.

The demand for passenger-carrying machines had never been greater. The overall increase in power

Two popular marques of the mid-1920s—and later—were Douglas (above) famous for flat-twins like this 1926 350cc model, and Francis-Barnett (below), whose 'Built like a Bridge' 1926 150cc two-stroke model featured a fully-triangulated frame

William G. Henderson was America's leading designer of four-cylinder machines. Apart from the Excelsior and the ACE, he also built machines under his own name, like this 1300cc model of the early 1920s (below). Reverse gear was an optional extra

Four-cylinder two-stroke: Professor A.M. Low's 1921 one-off experimental motor cycle

meant that all types of machine from around 250cc upwards could even cope with the added weight of sidecars. The sidecars designed for the smaller machines, although of reasonable streamline form, offered little more in the way of weather protection than pre-war examples, but makes such as the Canoelet and the Grindlay pioneered the fitting of windscreens and hoods as standard. Motor cycles of 8hp or so could deal with heavy closed sidecars built like midget motor bodies–in 1919–21 there was a shortlived vogue for the 'sidecar taxi', which failed to last, probably because of the type's limited carrying capacity.

Sidecar chassis design progressed slowly as suspension layouts improved, although the development of Millford in 1920 of the chassis-less Rock sidecar, had no lasting value.

Although the sidecar outfit remained popular throughout the 1920s–the Eccles Caravan Co even listed caravans to be towed by sidecar combinations–sales were definitely diminished by the advent of such excellent small cars as the Austin Seven, which offered far superior weather protection and comparable performance for much the same initial outlay.

So, as always, it was the solo machine which held the limelight–and anyway the advent of the pillion seat (or 'flapper bracket') first introduced pre-war by LMC, but popularised by the excellent Tan-Sad (tandem saddle) proprietory fitting, meant that the motor cyclist could carry a passenger in passable comfort.

Apart from the general improvements in engine and transmission design, the shape of the motor cycle was undergoing a fundamental change.

The frame, for example, which up to the outbreak of war was generally little better than a strengthened pushbike unit, had hitherto received scant attention. Scott, as usual, differed from the common herd, offering a strong fully triangulated duplex frame, with the engine playing a vital role in bracing the whole. The early 1920s saw many manufacturers following the Scott lead in duplicating the major frame tubes to give an exceptionally rigid construction.

Possibly nobody went further with the duplex frame idea than Willoughby Cotton from Gloucester, whose fully triangulated machines were a distinctive feature of the sporting scene for so many years. No fewer than eight frame tubes located the rear wheel, and six kept the steering head rigid; small wonder that the Cotton was famed for its roadholding.

At the same time, spring frame design was becoming neater and more effective, backed up by improved saddles, often with double springing, bigger tyres, of up to 3in in section, and better mudguards.

This accent on rider comfort prompted a revival of interest in the all-enclosed type of motor cycle. Small scooters were developed in profusion, but being usually underpowered, with one extremely low gear, were only suitable for local journeys, and the type rapidly became extinct.

It was less easy to understand the reason for the demise of the larger enclosed machines. These seemed to be the answer to the problem of providing a motor cycle for the masses, but after a brief success, sales of enclosed motor cycles fell away, despite efforts to re-introduce the concept during the 1920s.

One of the most advanced of these machines was the frameless pressed steel 500cc four-cylinder two-stroke Low, built in 1921–2, albeit as an experiment, not for production. Its designer, Professor A.M.Low, was a prolific writer on scientific subjects for the popular press, who also ran a laboratory at Feltham, Middlesex, 'where many war secrets were hatched'. Postwar projects included an automatic saucepan 'to boil eggs to perfection', 'wirelessing 1000 miles' and, 'one of his easiest ventures', building the foolproof motor cycle. But Low was too mercurial to continue with the project once he knew it worked.

Financial problems doomed the Pullin-Groom, designed by ex-TT rider Cyril Pullin. In production between 1920–25, the Pullin-Groom broke away completely from established principles. It had a pressed-steel frame and forks, with good weather protection, and was powered by Pullin's unorthodox 350cc two-stroke engine which dispensed with a carburettor completely, using a 'mixing-valve' to get the mixture into the cylinder.

A few years later Cyril Pullin tried again, with the Ascot-Pullin, which again made wide use of pressed steel. It featured a windscreen (with wiper), built-in instruments, legshields, hydraulic brakes and quickly detachable and interchangeable wheels.

At a selling price of £75, the 496cc Ascot-Pullin looked like a bargain, but few people cared for its advanced concept, and the machine was only built from 1928 to 1930.

But despite the excellence of designs like these, or the little Unibus built by Gloster Aircraft, only one all-enclosed machine really caught on during the 1920s, and that had its origins in the United States.

In 1921 the Ner-a-Car Corporation of Syracuse, New York, began production of an unorthodox machine designed by Carl Neracher. It had a pressed steel frame, with all the mechanism except the cylinder head enclosed, five-speed friction drive and 'forkless' hub-control steering, which the first British journalist to road test the machine claimed gave the Ner-a-Car, 'the same feeling of stickiness when leaning over on a corner that one experiences with a Scott'.

A production licence was granted to the British car manufacturers, Sheffield-Simplex, who built Ner-a-Cars, with a choice of the original 285cc two-stroke engine or more powerful Blackburne 350cc units, from late 1921 until 1926, when conventionality, as usual, won the day and the Ner-a-Car vanished from the scene.

Part of the reason for its demise, perhaps, was the

The ohv 500cc BSA sloper was introduced in 1926 and continued in production until 1935 in ohv and sv form, with cylinder capacities of 350cc, 500cc or 600cc. It had a duplex loop frame and cost less than £60

A short-lived venture of the post-Armistice years was the sidecar taxi, which only seated one passenger, limiting its usefulness. For virtually the same price the would-be taxi operator could buy a second hand closed car and drive in comfort . . .

Last of the great American motor cycles is the Harley Davidson, famed for big vee-twins for over 60 years. This late 1920s model (below) has many design features still recognisable in today's Harleys

This two-seated conversion of the Ner-a-Car dates from the end of the machine's five-year production run, and features ample weather protection

A real car on two wheels was the Monotrac of the mid-1920s, which had outrigged 'landing gear' to keep it upright when at a standstill

The 1920s saw a spate of enclosed and semi-enclosed designs, of which the 1928–30 Ascot-Pullin (above) was perhaps the most advanced, with pressed-steel frame, quick-change wheels and hydraulic brakes

Three scooters of the 1920s – the Reynolds Runabout (above) had a 269cc Liberty two-stroke engine and was built by former car maker R.Reynold Jackson, while the neat little Unibus (left), the work of a designer called Boultbee, was produced by the Gloster Aircraft Company. It had a car-type chassis and suspension. Its modern, fully-enclosed lines contrast strongly with its cruder contemporary, the Hagg Tandem (below)

growing practicality of the standard mount. Typical was the 1927 BSA 'sloper' single which covered 250 000 trouble-free miles in 32 years and was then returned to its makers for restoration. The Lucas Magdyno and ML Maglita combined electric ignition and generating sets meant that all types of machine could now have electric lighting. The demise of the acetylene lamp was fairly rapid, although a proportion of traditionalists still clung to the older system as they felt that to rely entirely on electricity was putting too many eggs in one basket.

The ability to ride further meant that the quaint old slab-shaped petrol tank was inadequate. The solution came from the racing world, in the shape of the bulbous saddle tank, which straddled the top tube of the frame, and gave almost double the fuel capacity. Some makers, like Sunbeam, clung desperately to the flat tank, but by the end of the 1920s the saddle tank was universal.

But all was not perfection, for the newer, faster and heavier bikes were prone to develop ailments that were unknown to their more sluggish ancestors. The most unpleasant of these was 'speed-wobble' where the front wheel suddenly shook violently from side to side in a fast-moving blur, which at worst could end in the machine going out of control. The empirical remedy was to fit a friction damper to the steering head, which the rider tightened down at speed.

Rudge-Whitworth attempted to make an apparent virtue out of this necessity by building a clock into the damper on their 1931 499cc Special.

However, road-holding in general was much improved, as new frame designs brought the saddle position – and the centre of gravity – lower, and as far as appearance and performance were concerned, the motor cycle of the late 1920s was not to be bettered for 20 years.

If there was one machine which encompassed all the virtues of that era, it was that superb production, the Brough Superior. Its beginnings had been inauspicious enough. In 1919 young George Brough had risen to hold a one-third share in his father's motor cycle manufacturing company in Basford, Nottingham. But he had a burning ambition, which his parent did not share, to build a super-luxury motor cycle. So he re-signed, and set up his own factory in Hayden Road, Nottingham. The first Brough Superiors, fitted with a '90 bore' vee-twin JAP-engine, were built in late 1919, and soon the marque, by virtue of its impeccable finish, earned itself the tag 'the Rolls Royce of motor cycles'.

Nevertheless the early Brough Superiors were merely assembled from bought-out components, generally specially built to Brough's specification.

Competition successes came early: and for 1923 a new speed model, the 988cc SS80 was introduced. The first racing SS80 – Spit and Polish, later renamed Old Bill – was the first sidevalve motor cycle to lap Brooklands at over 100mph, and in 1922–3 gained 51 firsts in a row.

At the 1924 Olympia Exhibition, George Brough unveiled an even more sporting model, the SS100, sold with a written 100mph guarantee. It was on 1925 SS100s that the Brough-built Castle front forks were first used; their sliding action gave far superior steering geometry to the conventional girder pattern. Out of the SS100 grew the Alpine Grand Sports, which sold at £170, and its racing version, the Pendine, catalogued at £165. A smaller version, the 680, by 1929 had become the Black Alpine, finished entirely in eggshell black.

T.E. Lawrence (Lawrence of Arabia) owned seven Broughs between 1922 and 1935, when he was killed swerving to avoid a careless boy cyclist. Lawrence described himself as 'not a speed merchant' but thought little of riding 500–700 miles in a day; eloquent testimony to the Brough's impeccable road manners.

It was, perhaps, the finest machine of the motor cycle's finest decade. The world-wide slide into financial chaos was to ensure that such a golden age would never occur again.

Motor cycling in rural Kent, 1921. The prototype Superb Four, ridden by designer L.F. Hooper, meets an AJS sidecar outfit

Going to the TT Races

Line-up at the start of the 1922 Senior TT, with (left to right) Triumph-Ricardo, Scott Squirrel, Douglas ohv flat-twin and side valve Norton. But Alec Bennett's side valve Sunbeam won the race

Racing, goes the aphorism, improves the breed. And the post-First World War TT Races really proved the point of that old saying.

In 1920, the first year after the Armistice that manufacturers were able to give their attention to preparing racing machines, the amateur with the ability to tune the engine of a standard production machine still stood an excellent chance of securing a place. Norton, whose policy was to race machines that were identical with those that customers could buy, had built 14 of the 27 starters in the Senior TT, five of the 14 being works entries.

Otherwise, there were five specially built and tuned Sunbeams, three Indians, two ABCs, a Douglas, a Duzmo and a 350cc AJS, which proved nearly as fast as the 500cc machines.

The roads were atrocious, virtually all unmade cart tracks, the suspension of most of the competing machines was nugatory, and the riders had a miserable time keeping their cycles on the road. Brakes were still mostly the ineffective pull-up pushbike type, although Sunbeam used dummy belt rims, the brake block being forced into the 'V' of the belt. The Indians dispensed with front brakes altogether!

The fastest machines were the Sunbeams, thanks to the use of aluminium pistons, rather than the cast-iron type in normal use, and an advanced lubrication system, but the Nortons had a primitive form of foot gearchange, and the race was extremely close. De la Hay (Sunbeam) beat Brown (Norton) by $3\frac{1}{2}$ minutes. In eleventh place was Black on a privately-entered Norton, the last belt-drive machine ever to finish a Senior TT.

In 1921 eleven manufacturers entered 68 machines, many specially built, but the advance in engine design was dramatically shown when Howard Davies on a 350cc AJS came in first, ahead of Indians ridden by Freddie Dixon and Bert Le Vack.

An identical machine ridden by Eric Williams won the Junior TT. The ease with which the 'Ajays' handled contributed in no small manner to their success, for the 500s scaled 250–300lb as opposed to the 202lb all-up weight of the AJS, which cornered better than any other machine in the race. But there were complaints that 'the AJS machines were special and could not be

obtained or possibly even ridden by the public'.

The 1922 Senior saw the first TT victory for the great rider Alec Bennett, who also won the fastest road race yet run, the 1922 French Grand Prix at 61mph, and who was to win four more TTs before he retired. In the TT the engine of his Sunbeam was almost completely ruined by lack of oil – it was a miracle that it finished at all, but nevertheless Bennett set up a new record race average of 58·33mph. His machine was the last side-valve single to win a TT.

The Junior that year was won by the first of the immortal 'Big Port' ohv AJS, offspring of Davies' 1921 Senior victor, and one of the most famous racing motor cycles ever built.

In 1923 the first sidecar TT was held, and won by that unique character Freddie Dixon, at the helm of a 596cc Douglas outfit fitted with a banking sidecar of his own design to aid cornering; Dixon crossed the line holding the sidecar steady with his foot, for the chassis had broken in three places, the cycle frame in two. His average for the race was an astounding 53·15mph.

It was a Douglas year in 1923, for Sheard won the Senior on a 'Duggie' at 55·55mph in pouring rain;

Norton was one of the greatest names in Tourist Trophy racing. Their run of successes began in 1924 with Alec Bennett's victory at 61·64mph

his mount was not only the lightest '500' (257lb) in the race, it was also the most advanced technically, the specification including 'disc' brakes. It had been designed and built in under five months and had come to the Isle of Man virtually untried.

This TT established the superiority of overhead valve designs, and saw the tentative introduction of steering dampers to improve roadholding.

Several leading manufacturers decided not to enter works teams in the 1924 Senior, as the cost of competing in five races – Senior, Junior, Lightweight, Ultra Lightweight and Sidecar TTs – in one week was prohibitive. Alec Bennett's ohv Norton won the race at 61·64mph in front of a huge and enthusiastic crowd. The patriarchal James L.'Pa' Norton, in poor health for many years, had literally kept himself alive by the will to repeat Fowler's 1907 victory. Now that the feat had been accomplished, he died happy in the following year.

Freddie Dixon's banking sidecar Douglas outfit won the 1923 Sidecar TT with the frame broken in two places, the sidecar chassis in three, held together by Dixon's foot!

The enthusiasm engendered by the 1924 race caused the manufacturers to rethink their policy regarding works entries, and 48 machines from 12 makers started in the 1925 Senior, only to be soundly trounced by Howard Davies riding an HRD of his own design and manufacture, one of a small batch of machines built in Davies' little factory in Wolverhampton. His average speed was 66·13mph. Parker (Douglas) won the last Sidecar TT for 14 years, which was held in 1925.

In 1926 Stanley Woods (Norton) won the Senior at 67·54mph, while in 1927 Alec Bennett took first place at 68·41mph on a new overhead camshaft 500cc Norton, based on the design work of Walter Moore. This model then went into production as the CS 1. But other manufacturers were keeping pace with Norton.

Torrential rain reduced the average speed of the 1928 winner, Dodson (Sunbeam) to 62·98mph, although he won the next year's Senior at a speed virtually 10mph faster, becoming the first TT winner to average over 70mph.

During the 1920s such famous events as the Dutch TT and the Belgian, German, Italian and Ulster Grands Prix, were first run. In these races, the three main capacity classes, 500cc, 350cc and 250cc, usually raced together, as there were too few competitors to make up full fields in any one class.

Although the Tourist Trophy was the premier race of the 1920s, in Britain Brooklands played an important part in the development of the motor cycle, especially where high speed records were concerned. A major landmark occurred in 1920, when D.H.Davidson became the first rider to exceed 100mph, mounted, appropriately enough, on a Harley-Davidson. During practice for the run his light racing saddle collapsed and jammed the back wheel; the machine proceeded sideways for a considerable distance at high speed.

An even more spectacular machine was the mighty 1000cc Temple-Anzani ohc vee-twin designed by Hubert Hagens, which first appeared in May 1923. Very fast, and with a short wheelbase which made the machine hard to handle, the Temple-Anzani was originally painted pale purple with yellow wheels. Its performance, in the hands of its gifted rider Claude Temple, was equally brilliant: by July 1923 it was lapping at 104·85mph, and had set up new standing start five and ten mile records of 104·31 and 101·15mph respectively. It was not the first machine to lap the track at over 100mph, however, that honour belongs to

Graham Walker (Rudge) leads Charlie Dodson (Sunbeam) in the 1928 Senior Ulster Grand Prix

Three famous racers of the 1920s. Tom Sheard (above) won the 1923 Senior TT on this disc-braked Douglas, in a torrential rainstorm. Claude Temple's Temple-Anzani (below) was one of the fastest Brooklands machines of the decade, capable of lap speeds well in excess of 100mph. Norton's CS1 500cc ohc model (right) won the 1927 Senior TT at a record 68·41mph, ridden by Alec Bennett

Bert Le Vack's big Zenith, which achieved it in 1922 – and in the wet!

The first 100mph lap of the track by a 500cc machine was made in 1925 by Bert Le Vack on a New Hudson, who exceeded the magic 'ton' by a hundredth part of an mph.

H. J. Knight lapped at over 110mph in 1925, and by 1929 the record stood at 118·86mph, set by Wright (Brough Superior). The famous rider-tuner C. W. G. Lacey covered 103·3 miles in an hour in August 1928, while Ernie Nott travelled 200·46 miles in two hours on a 500cc Rudge.

Motor cycle racing was a major part of the Brooklands scene, too. In the 1920s, the track was the base for a number of works riders who raced all season through: Bertie Newsome and Freddy Edmonds (Triumphs); George Dance and Greenwood (Sunbeams); T. C. de la Hay and G. W. Patchett (McEvoys); Victor Horsman and Bert Le Vack with JAP-engined machines; Cyril Pullin (Douglas); Glovers and Worters (Excelsior); and Rex Judd and D. R. 'Wizard' O'Donovan with Nortons.

I met Rex Judd towards the end of his life, many years later. Ill though he was, he still recalled Brooklands with pleasure. He first went there during the First World War, for one of the 'All-Khaki' meetings restricted to members of the armed forces. Then, in 1920, he was engaged in breaking long distance records on Coulson B (for Blackburne engines) belt-driven sidecar combinations at the track.

In 1921, Judd joined Norton Motorcycles, where his task was to pass out 28 machines a month with a guaranteed speed of 70 or 75mph at Brooklands. These were marketed as the models BS and BRS.

Rex Judd also went in for long-distance record-breaking on Nortons, including the 24 hour stint, in company with Victor Horsman. On the second day, Judd covered 700 miles at an average speed of some 62mph.

On March 29, 1921, Rex Judd, riding a 3½hp Norton,

Typical racing sidecar outfit of the mid-1920s – Simpson's 350cc AJS TT outfit of 1925, with its airship-styled sidecar

won the Godfrey Cup, awarded for the first man to exceed 90mph on a 500cc machine (his actual speed was 92·44mph). There were, in fact, three Godfrey Cups, awarded in memory of O.C.Godfrey by the motor cycle dealership he had founded. They were for the first 350cc machine to do 80mph; the first 500cc machine to do 90mph; and the first machine under 1000cc to exceed 100mph. The other two Cups were won by H.R.Davies on October 19, 1920, on a 2¾hp AJS (80·47mph) and D.H.Davidson on a 7·8hp Harley-Davidson (100·46mph). Davidson's record was, however, not destined to stand for long, as on the following day, April 29, 1921, Bert Le Vack, riding a 7·9hp Indian, covered the flying kilometre at 106·52mph.

Rex Judd, who continued racing at Brooklands until the end of 1927, transferred to Douglas in 1922, joining the brilliant designer-rider Cyril Pullin, and remained with that company until he gave up racing. With

In 1921 D.R.'Wizard' O'Donovan took the sidecar flying kilometre record on this side valve Norton at 72·36mph

Douglas, he broke many records, mostly short distances of up to 10 miles.

'The best race I had was the 200 mile event of 1924', he told me, 'when five of us kept together for an hour, and no-one led for more than two laps. Unfortunately, we all fell out one after another, but the first hour was exceptionally good fun'.

The 200 miler, though, was nothing compared with the longest two-wheeler race ever held at Brooklands, the 500 mile event of 1921. Winner was Bert Le Vack, riding an Indian, followed by Freddie Dixon on a Harley-Davidson and Reuben Harveyson on another Indian. Le Vack's average was 70·42mph.

But local residents thought the race created too much noise, and it was abandoned. From the riders' point of view this was probably as well, for 500 miles on a two-wheeler over the rough concrete of Brooklands was a purgatorial experience.

Another man who well remembered Brooklands in the 1920s was Bob Dicker, who once held twenty-two world records, many taken on a belt-drive Zenith-Gradua.

'Taking records was very tiring', he commented. 'You see, you had no shock absorbers, you had no steering dampers, and small tyres . . . you had to fight it round'.

One of the great secrets was knowing how to ride the track, and this was something that could only be learned by years of experience.

'No three laps would be the same. If the wind changed you'd ride a different course. If it was blowing hard, across the track, I would come right down the bank and let all the aviation sheds protect me, then if it was blowing hard the other way, I'd go up the bank a bit so that the wind would go over the top of me. All that made a difference of about three miles an hour. That's only for record-breaking – you couldn't do that in racing, you hadn't got time.

When you are out for records, you are continually working all the time, although it seems to the onlookers that you're just sitting there having a good time, but no-one knows what you're thinking, and you're thinking and working the whole time. After a couple of hours you'd get a terrific ache in your arms and your knees – you did your steering with your knees – and when we first used crash helmets they made our necks ache terribly, because we weren't used to all that load up there.

When they showed you a golden can, you came in for some petrol, and after you'd had that small stop of 35 seconds, those aches all went, and they didn't come on again for an hour. Just 30 seconds rest, and it got rid of all those aches and pains – but when they came back they were worse than ever!'

Prior to 1909, American motor cycle races were generally held on moderately banked board cycle tracks, but these soon proved inadequate for the rapid eight-valve Harley-Davidsons and Indians, and following a gory accident when several machines left the track simultaneously, killing eight spectators, the use of board tracks declined.

Speedway racing came to Britain from Australia in 1928 and soon became a craze

been established, where the 'speed demons' could participate in the new sport.

By 1936 speedway racing was holding a world championship, and it continues to this day to be a keenly-contested sport with a considerable following, in which it is the rider rather than his machine which counts.

Almost from the dawn of the motor cycle era speed trials and hillclimbs on the public highway – with the local police turning a benevolently blind eye to the proceedings – had been a prominent feature of the sport, especially in England and France. In the early 1920s in England this form of competition reached its peak, and it was in these events that the TT riders learned their secrets of tune.

Most prominent of the post-war riders was George Dance, whose ohv 350cc and 500cc Sunbeams were virtually unbeatable. He would arrive at the venue in style with a motor cycle on either running board of his Cubitt car and a sidecar in the tonneau. With the 500 he often took the premier award in every class over the period 1919–22, but lost his winning form after a bad crash.

Among his strongest competitors were 'Fiery' Fred Dixon, mounted on a rapid four-valves-per-cylinder 1000cc vee-twin Harley-Davidson, Bert Le Vack on an eight-valve Indian and E. C. Baragwanath and I.P.Riddoch on mammoth Zenith-Gradua JAPs.

But the exciting era of the public road sprint and hillclimb came to a sudden end in 1925 when a Bugatti car went off the road and injured a spectator at Kop Hill, near Princes Risborough in Buckinghamshire, and the RAC and ACU slapped an instant ban on such events.

Only a few sand race meetings on the wide beaches of such resorts as Pendine and Southport survived, and support for these events declined rapidly. Otherwise, sprint meetings were restricted to private grounds, and these events never had the same romantic, slightly illegal, atmosphere as the public road contests.

Then the racers turned their attention to the loose-surfaced horse trotting tracks, developing a spectacular broadsiding method of riding – by 1913 the one-mile dirt-track record stood at over 83mph. The new sport spread to Canada, where the 16-year-old Alec Bennett won his first professional race on the Vancouver dirt-track in 1913, riding a self-tuned Indian.

From Canada, dirt-track racing had reached Australia, where it gained a sizable following, sufficient to encourage two leading Australian riders, Billy Galloway and Keith McKay, to risk their 1927 season's winnings on an attempt to introduce the sport into England.

In February 1928 an estimated 30 000 spectators crowded around the tiny quarter-mile cinder track specially constructed behind the King's Oak public house at High Beech, Epping Forest. The meeting was a huge success . . . 'some of the competitors leaned over and trailed their left boot, shod with steel, in the dirt . . . it looked exciting, but the average speed was not more than 40mph.' Soon some 50 tracks had

The dapper George Dance and his 2½hp ohv Sunbeam were an unbeatable combination in the hill climbs of 1919–20

Another famous machine of the early 1920s was the Zenith-Blackburne ridden by I.P.Riddoch, which won the last 'open road' sprint

Down the Hill to Disaster

The Depression had caused output figures to plummet downwards – British production fell from 146 715 in 1929 to 126 524 in 1930, plunged to 75 031 in 1931 and finally bottomed in 1933 at 52 205 yet there was no lack of new designs.

At the 1929 Motor Cycle Show Matchless introduced a splendid touring machine, the side-valve 397cc Silver Arrow, with the cylinders arranged in a narrow vee, with a 26 degree angle between them, giving the compact appearance of a vertical twin. It was the harbinger of an even more original design, the 597cc Silver Hawk, which had an overhead camshaft vee-four-cylinder engine with only 18 degrees between the cylinders; this gave a short, rigid crankshaft, and kept the engine short enough to fit inside a conventional duplex frame, with pivoted rear springing.

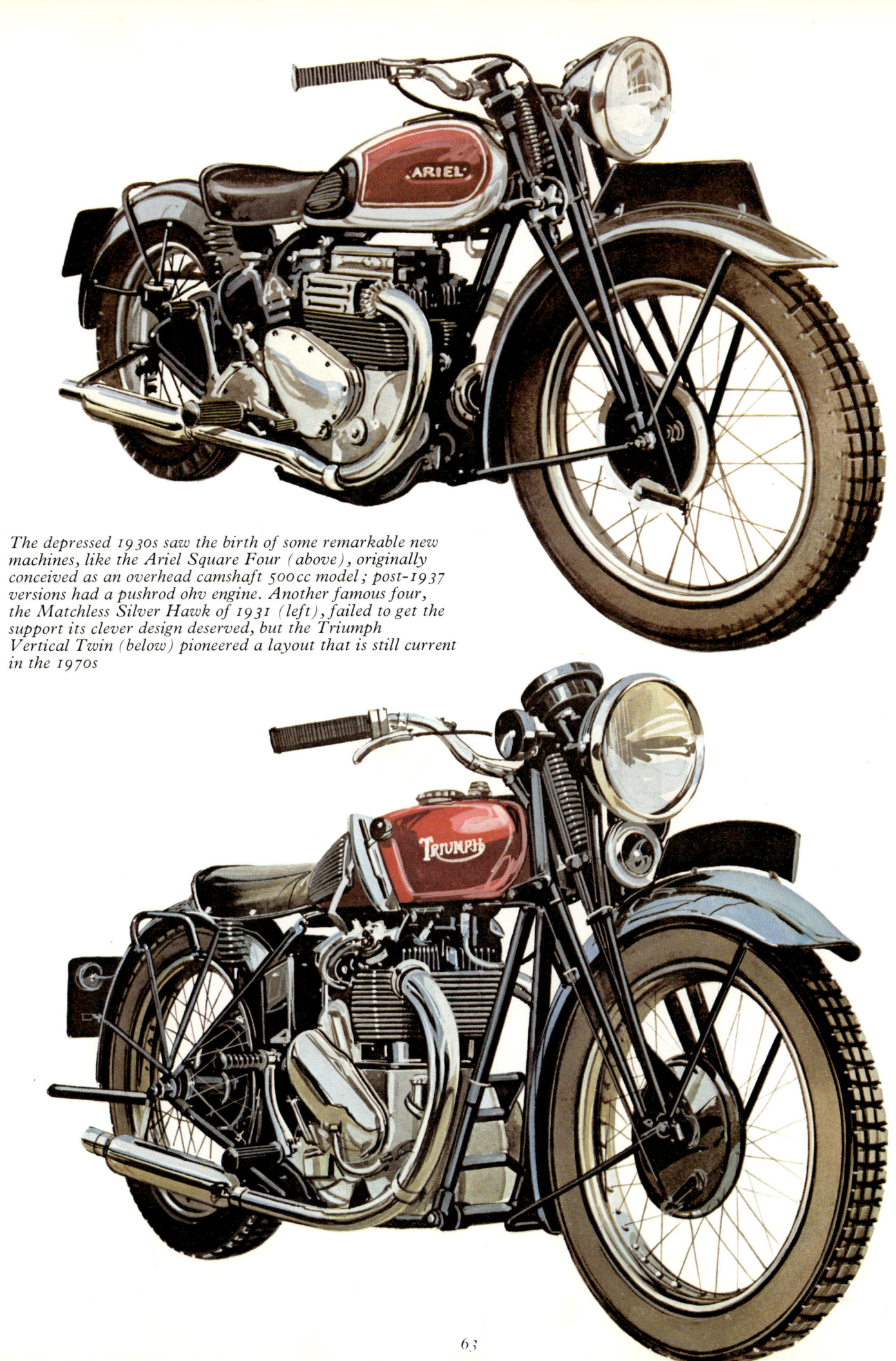

The depressed 1930s saw the birth of some remarkable new machines, like the Ariel Square Four (above), originally conceived as an overhead camshaft 500cc model; post-1937 versions had a pushrod ohv engine. Another famous four, the Matchless Silver Hawk of 1931 (left), failed to get the support its clever design deserved, but the Triumph Vertical Twin (below) pioneered a layout that is still current in the 1970s

'Acceleration, comfort and superb silence' were the chief attractions of the Silver Hawk, according to Arthur Bourne, 'Torrens' of *The Motor Cycle*, who owned a 1932 Silver Hawk, accounting his ownership as 'the most enjoyable riding of my life' in a test report published after the first 5 000 miles. 'Sheer out-and-out speed is not the Hawk's strongest suit', he wrote. 'It will put just over eighty on the special "police test" speedometer if one gets down to it, and 76 to 78mph with the rider sitting up. The great point, though, is that Hawk's speed can be used. Bumps it sails over by reason of the very efficient, trouble-free spring frame, and sixty or more can be maintained over poorish roads without the rider being thrown about, or the machine seeking to run wild.

'The steering is magnificent at all except very low speeds, when it is on the heavy side, and the cornering is like that of a first-class TT mount'.

Even these outstanding qualities–coupled with a £75 price tag–failed to gain the Silver Hawk a large enough share of the market: and the model was discontinued after 1935.

But a subsequent multi-cylinder addition to the Bourne stable, a 1 000cc Ariel Square Four, was perhaps the most successful four-cylinder model of all time.

'It corners like a 500, has the power of a Senior TT mount and the good manners of just about as docile a tourer as has ever been made', enthused 'Torrens' in 1936.

In fact the 'Squariel', designed by Edward Turner, had originally been a 500 when it was introduced in 1929.

The 490cc engine was basically two parallel twins with their flywheels geared together so that they revolved in opposite directions, giving excellent balance and smoothness.

Other features of the design–uprated to 600cc in 1935–were a monobloc cylinder block and a chain driven overhead camshaft. But when the final capacity increase, to 1 000cc, was made in 1936, the camshaft was supplanted by pushrods. With the occasional modernisation, the Square Four survived in production in this form right up to 1958.

Although it was usually attached to family sidecars, the big Ariel was no slouch in solo form: a blown 500cc version, tuned and ridden by Ben Bickell, proved capable of lapping Brooklands at 112mph in 1934, despite a tendency to blow gaskets.

The Square Four's future was not always unclouded. In mid-1932 the Ariel factory was within an ace of closing down permanently, but in October it was announced that the company was back in operation, and within twelve months recovery was complete enough for the firm to undertake a major expansion.

Triumph had been losing money heavily in the 1930s, and blamed the losses squarely on its motor cycle activities. So Edward Turner persuaded Jack Y. Sangster, managing director of Ariel, that the ailing Triumph business would be a worthwhile acquisition, and the two companies joined forces.

One of Triumph's leading models was a 650cc

Climbing the Beggars Roost test hill on a shaft-driven 500cc Douglas Endeavour in the winter of 1935

vertical twin designed by Val Page. Turner continued the vertical twin theme, and his 1937 Speedtwin was one of the classic motor cycle designs. A 350cc version followed soon after.

The enthusiasm aroused by the Speedtwin was terrific. A New York agent ordered one of the first production batches, sensing a keen demand for the new model. Yet by the time he had paid freight and import duties, the machines cost as much as a 20hp six-cylinder car. But they sold!

That Turner's decision to acquire Triumph was the right one was shown by the fact that the company broke even the first year after the takeover and made a handsome profit the next, becoming established once again as one of the major British manufacturers.

But though the twins and fours were the machines that made the headlines, the typical British production machine was, as it had always been, a vertical single side-valver of between 150cc and 600cc, with a moderate compression ratio that encouraged flexibility.

Design improvements had gained a little extra power, but, as so often happens, the machines had put on extra weight, which meant that there was little gain in performance. Typically, a 1938 500 scaled around 400lb, twice the weight of a model of similar capacity in the early 1920s.

However, reliability was much improved; the old spit-and-miss total-loss lubrication system had been supplanted by the cleaner, more positive, mechanical pump and dry-sump method; oil-scraper piston rings cut down oil consumption and increased the period between decokes; detachable cylinder heads replaced the old all-in-one cylinders and simplified servicing. And engines were cleaner, thanks to the casing-in of the valve gear. From the viewpoint of ease of control, the standardisation of twistgrip throttle control and foot gear change in the early 1930s was a major step forward. So was the growing adoption of rear springing and well-base tyres.

But not all the developments of the 1930s were such positive benefits. There was, for example, a trend towards mounting the instruments and switches in a panel on the top of the petrol tank, rather than on the steering head. It may have tidied away some of the electric wiring, but on just about every other count it was, claimed one keen motor cyclist 'the most ridiculous motor cycle fashion of all time'.

Most annoying of all was the rats-nest of wiring exposed when the tank was removed for routine maintenance, when the leads all had to be disconnected and labelled. . . .

Despite all these changes, the motor cycles of the 1930s were stereotyped in appearance. Although rear springing was more in evidence, it added to production costs, so the economy machines of the period retained the solid rear ends.

These low-cost machines were a product of the Depression; to make any inroad on the market, prices had to be fixed at almost giveaway levels. There was brave talk in 1931 of marketing a £12 'utility' machine for the working man, and this flight of fancy was little removed from the truth. In 1933 you could buy a fully-equipped 150cc machine for £19 19s. Another couple of pounds saw to the legal formalities, and you were away on the open road.

Yet these little machines were far from toys. It was possible for two people to make a 2000 mile, two-week tour of the Continent on a 150cc motor cycle for a total cost of under £25, without any of the breakdowns that would have plagued a lightweight of the mid-1920s.

By this time, the two-stroke engine had become almost universal at the lower end of the capacity range, thanks to improved power, and increased freedom from the old bugbear of plug whiskering.

In the main this was due to the pioneering work of Doctor Schnuerle in Germany; his designs did away with the old 'deflector' on top of the piston which nudged the gas in the right direction across the cylinder, and used a flat-topped piston and angled ports to give the correct gas-flow. The British firm of Villiers adopted Schnuerle's ideas, and soon their entire range,

Full enclosure was a feature of the 1934 Vincent HRD Model W, too, with its 250cc water-cooled power unit concealed by castings

from 98cc to 350cc used flat-topped pistons. And in 1935 they produced 98cc and 125cc engines built in unit with a clutch and three-speed gearbox, a layout which eventually became standard.

Villiers engines were virtually universal on lightweight machines—especially on the low-powered, open-frame autocycles, simple two-speeders with pedalling gear and played a major part in promoting the 'Everyman Utility' machine. Easily started and handled by the novice, the Everyman machine was designed to be silent, flexible and comfortable, with adequate weather protection, and simple to clean and maintain.

One outcome was the attempt to produce a motor cycle that could be hosed down as easily as a car, by partial enclosure of the mechanism, the more difficult-to-clean components such as the gearbox being concealed beneath pressed-steel panels.

Vincent-HRD, who were to become firmly established as makers of super-luxury machines in the Brough-Superior class, offered a neat 250cc Villiers two-stroke-powered machine in which a special cast aluminium silencer formed the nose of a pressing enclosing all the mechanism bar the cylinder barrel. Francis-Barnett carried the same theme (with the same power unit) to greater lengths on their 1933 Cruiser, the pressed-steel frame of which incorporated leg-shields.

Perhaps it was shame, as much as fashion, which caused Douglas to conceal the fact that their 150cc Bantam utility model of 1932 had a vertical single Villiers engine—not the make's characteristic flat-twin—behind pressed steel panels.

At the top end of the two-stroke market, Scott continued to develop their old water-cooled parallel-twin engine. However, in 1935 they built the prototype of an advanced 750cc in-line unit, with a built-up crank-

Full enclosure masked the fact that the 1933 Douglas Bantam was powered by a 150cc two-stroke engine and not the traditional flat-twin

Winner of the last pre-war Senior TT was George Meier's
BMW (left) which had a supercharger mounted on the front
of the crankshaft of its 500cc ohc flat-twin engine,
full-width hubs and telescopic front forks. But it was the
last supercharged machine to win the TT, for after the war
the international racing rules were altered to exclude blowers,
and BMW had to revise their designs
Horizontal opposition was a feature of the 1938 Brough
Superior Golden Dream (above) which had a flat-four
engine with its two crankshafts geared together for
maximum smoothness. However, only six examples of this
997cc luxury bike were built to special order before
Brough Superior ceased production

shaft running on ball and roller bearings. Intended for use in light cars as well as motor cycles, it was abandoned due to lack of finance.

The real leader in the two-stroke field remained Germany, where DKW were putting Schnuerle's ideas into practice with a range which included 248cc and 350cc singles and a 500cc twin. More importantly, they were developing special racing designs, including a version with a separate supercharger pump to force the fuel into the cylinder. A blown 248cc DKW – fast, noisy and thirsty – touched the marque's peak of success when it carried off the 1938 Lightweight TT at a speed of 78·48mph.

Other German two-strokes of advanced design were the Zundapp, Victoria and Imperia models, which paved the way to increased acceptance of the two-stroke on the Continent.

As far as four-strokes went, BMW continued to develop their horizontally-opposed twin with shaft drive, which had already become a classic model. Another distinguished German design of the 1930s was the 797cc Zundapp of 1933, which had a pressed-steel frame and shaft drive. Only its styling was clumsy.

A pressed-steel frame was also a feature of one of the few four-cylinder designs to become popular outside Britain in the 1930s. This was the 750cc ohv Nimbus from Denmark, which had originally appeared

Ewald Kluge rode this 248cc DKW (above) to victory in the 1938 lightweight TT. It had a supercharged 'twingle' two-stroke engine – twin cylinders with a common combustion chamber

More conventional was the 1935 Rudge 499cc Ulster, developed from that firm's racing models, seen here getting down to some rapid lappery at Brooklands

in the 1920s. The new version had an improved engine, built in unit with the gearbox, and shaft final drive – and the whole machine scaled only 380lb. In America, of course, the old 1265cc Indian 4, *née* Ace, was still going strong; it remained in production until 1941.

But it was a British manufacturer, Brough Superior, which produced the outstanding four-cylinder machine of the decade.

Similar in concept to Edward Turner's Squariel, but costing more than twice as much, the 1938 Brough Superior Golden Dream was powered by a 997cc engine laid out as two superimposed flat-twins, with the crankshafts geared together to give well-nigh perfect balance. Final drive was by shaft and worm gear and there was a choice of three- or four-speed gearboxes.

Brough had tried to break away from the vee-twin before, in 1931, with a cumbersome looking shaft-driven in-line four powered by a modified Austin Seven engine of 800cc, equipped with twin rear wheels, but the Golden Dream showed this up as an example of misdirected ingenuity.

Unfortunately only half-a-dozen Dreams were built to bespoke order before war work brought Brough Superior production to an end.

The war ended one of the most remarkable eras of motor cycle sport, too, which had opened with one of the most memorable team victories of all time.

There had been instances before the 1930 Junior TT of makes taking the first three places in the event – but never had the hat-trick been achieved with three experimental models which had not even been road-tested before they were shipped to the Isle of Man.

This was the remarkable feat accomplished by Rudge-Whitworth, whose new 350cc design had a hemispherical combustion chamber accommodating four inclined valves – two inlet, two exhaust – actuated by two pushrods and six rockers. The winning machine, ridden by H. G. Tyrell Smith, averaged 71·08mph, the first time the 70mph average had been exceeded in the Junior; within 58 seconds, the second and third Rudges had passed the post.

And in the Senior race five days later, 500cc Rudges came first, second, sixth and seventh. The winning machine was ridden by Wal Handley, who had only joined the team a week before the race, having been let down by FN of Belgium at the last minute.

The weather was atrociously wet, yet Handley's average of 74·24mph was faster than the 1929 record lap. Third machine home was Jimmy Simpson's new overhead camshaft Norton, designed by Joe Craig. From 1931 on this 'cammy' Norton was all but invincible in the Senior TT – machines powered by developments of this engine won in 1931–34, 1936–38, 1947–54 and finally in 1961. The gaps in the 1930s were filled, significantly, by European designs, Moto Guzzi in 1935 and BMW in 1939.

The Guzzi which won the 1935 Senior was ridden by Stanley Woods. Jimmy Guthrie (Norton) had led for the first six laps, and actually finished ahead of Woods; while he was being congratulated on his win, Woods came roaring in to win by 4 seconds on elapsed time.

His mount, the first foreign machine to win a Senior since the 1911 Indian victory, had a wide-angle 120 degree ohc vee-twin engine with the forward cylinder carried horizontally to lower the centre of gravity and aid cooling of the rear cylinder, which developed a phenomenal 51bhp at 7500rpm. It was the first machine with a fully-sprung frame to win the Senior TT.

George Meier's 1939 winning BMW was also rear-sprung, and was exceptionally modern in appearance,

The earliest Danish Nimbus fours had tubular frames with the round tank forming the backbone. In the 1930s this model appeared, still using shaft drive, but with a pressed steel frame. The marque survived until 1957

Once a leading British maker of touring motor cycles, Calthorpe of Birmingham were especially famous for their 'Ivory' range of the 1930s (500cc model, above). But in 1938 the company went into liquidation, and an attempt by Bruce Douglas of Bristol to revive the name in 1939 was thwarted by the outbreak of war

Another honoured name of the period, Cotton, produced this sporting 490cc JAP-engined model (left), incorporating the fully-triangulated frame for which the company was famous. Founded in 1913, the Cotton Motor Company of Gloucester was still in limited production sixty years later

Founded even earlier, in 1900, Royal Enfield started production with De Dion type tricycles. Their proud slogan 'Built like a Gun' led, naturally to a range of models called 'Bullets'. This example (left) is the 489cc ohv Bullet 70 of the mid-1930s

AJS had been acquired by the Collier brothers in 1931, so Matchless knowhow was behind the company's advanced racers of the period. This supercharged, water-cooled V-4 appeared in 1939, but seems to have been too complex for its own good . . .

Based on the design of the mid-1930s Rondine, the 500cc Gilera Four of 1939 had a transverse engine with twin overhead camshafts. It was the principal rival to the V-4 AJS in the 1939 Ulster Grand Prix, a race which saw the 'Ajay' set up the first 100mph lap of the course, only to drop out with a broken chain link. The Gilera won at 98·85mph

with telescopic front forks and full-width wheel hubs. It had a 500cc ohc flat twin engine, which was super-charged. The blower was carried on the nose of the crankshaft.

BMW were no strangers to supercharging: in 1929 a blown 750cc BMW, carefully streamlined, covered a flying mile at 136·8mph, setting a new world record. A geared-down Zoller supercharger was fitted, and helped boost power, even with a moderate compression ratio, to 75bhp–100bhp per litre–and that from a pushrod engine!

But 1939 was the last year that supercharging was allowed. After the Second World War BMW had to modify the design to run unblown.

Some of the most remarkable supercharged machines of the period were the 'Big Blown Broughs', the first of which was built in 1930 by E.C.E. Baragwanath, and fitted with a Powerplus supercharged 1000cc vee-twin JAP engine, and which was capable–with a sidecar patterned after the float of the Supermarine Schneider Trophy racing seaplane–of over 110mph.

After Baragwanath retired, in 1933, at the age of 50, his machine was acquired by Noel Pope, who had cut his racing teeth on the old 996cc British Vulpine Anzani-powered Temple-OEC. Pope fitted an even more potent 1000cc JAP, and in this form the machine was capable of around 160mph solo, was the first to lap Brooklands at two miles a minute, and in 1939 set up the ultimate two-wheeler lap of Brooklands of 124·51mph. Five months later the track closed for ever, an incalculable loss to the racing world.

The other great Brough exponent of the era was Eric Fernihough, whose streamlined machine was Zoller-blown and set up the highest official two-wheeler speed–143·39mph–ever recorded at Brooklands. In 1937 Fernihough took the world speed record at 169·8mph at Gyon, Hungary. In an attempt to raise this figure the following year, he was blown off-course into a tree at over 180mph and killed.

DKW produced some pump-supercharged racing two-strokes in the late 1930s, but the real high-point of the supercharger era came in the 1939 Ulster Grand Prix, when Walter Rusk on the mighty 500cc ohc vee-four AJS, hitherto plagued by cooling troubles, set up the first 100mph lap of the course, only to drop out with a broken chain-link after a battle royal with Serafini's transverse four-cylinder twin ohc Gilera, which had engine, gearbox and supercharger in one gloriously engineered unit; the Italian won at an impressive record speed of 97·85mph.

War on Wheels

If the onset of the First World War had found Britain somewhat less than prepared as far as mechanisation was concerned, September 1939 found the British Forces in possession of over 21 000 motor cycles, with an Army Motor Cycling Control Board set up in 1938 in charge of the training of their riders.

Production continued apace, concentrated on simple, powerful, rugged single-cylinder sidevalve machines for communications and convoy patrol work. By June 1940 almost 50 000 two-wheelers were in service, this number being more than quintupled by VE Day. Ariel, BSA, Matchless, Norton, Royal Enfield and Triumph were the principal suppliers, their products being almost exclusively big singles of 350cc or 500cc capacity. BSA alone supplied over 100 000 machines for military use. James and Royal Enfield produced 125cc lightweights to be dropped by parachute with airborne troops while the Research Station at Welwyn designed the collapsible 98cc Welbike for a similar role; after the war a 'civilian' version was sold as the Corgi.

One war casualty was Triumph's 3TW, designed as the ideal military motor cycle at the request of the War Office. This 350cc machine weighed under 250lb, and the fuel tank formed a box girder. However, the initial production batch at Coventry was destroyed in an air raid, and development ceased.

Germany was highly motor cycle conscious, too, and the Wehrmacht made prolific use of heavy sidecar combinations, some with driven sidecar wheels, most capable of taking a machine gun or a mortar. Big BMWs (captured examples were copied by the Russians as the M72, still in service in the late 1960s) and 250cc NSU, DKWs and (German) Triumphs were among the solo mounts; BMW and Zundapp powered the sidecar outfits. Perhaps the most extraordinary design to see service with the Wehrmacht was the NSU Kettenkrad, a light motor cycle tractor fitted with half-tracks and powered by a 1·4 litre four-cylinder Opel car engine.

Italy's military motor cycles were notably more sporting than those of other combatant nations—captured Guzzis and Gileras were popular with British soldiers!

While America produced thousands of militarised Indians and Harleys, during the course of hostilities many of the functions performed by these machines were taken over by the Jeep.

The NSU Kettenkrad was one of the most extraordinary motor cycles of the Second World War, with its half-track drive. It was powered by a 1·4 litre Opel car engine

Towards the Superbiking Seventies

The shortage of raw materials and fuel after the war meant that economy was a prime feature of many designs, although selling prices were two or three times greater than in 1939. One of the greatest post-war motor cycles however was an extremely expensive luxury machine built to the most exacting standards.

The Vincent Rapide cost up to £474 and was the last of the classic vee-twins. It had a massively-built 998cc engine forming the main centre section of the frame.

In standard form the Vincent was capable of around 120mph; a modified version exceeded 160mph at Bonneville, Utah, in the early 1950s.

Suspension of the Vincent was hydraulically-damped girder forks at the front, and a pivoting rear end; detail design was impeccable, and the external finish was predominately black. A 500cc single was also made.

In 1954 Vincent announced their series D range, which featured glass-fibre fully-enclosed bodywork.

One of the great names in sidecar racing in the 1950s was BMW. These German flat-twin, shaft-drive machines had come a long way from their ABC origins. This is the type of low-built 'Kneeler' type streamliner that kept the marque out in front of its rivals

The AJS Porcupine of the late 1940s (above), with its unusual spine-cooled cylinder head, could have been a success, but somehow it was always plagued by minor troubles. A decade after the Porcupine, the Japanese moved in, with machines like Mike Hailwood's Honda (below)

Capable of cruising at speeds in the region of 100mph, the 1954 Vincent Black Prince was the last of the great British vee-twin roadburners. Vincent ceased production in 1956, although subsequent attempts to revive the name have been made

These models – the 998cc Black Prince and Black Knight and the 499cc Victor – were the sensation of the 1954 show, and were perhaps the most attractive all-enclosed models to be made up to that time (the German Horex Regina shown at the 1952 Geneva Show had shown how hideous full enclosure could look!).

But the Vincents were not just good lookers – the Black Prince was capable of 90–100mph cruising speeds, at a fuel consumption of over 50 miles per gallon, and had excellent roadholding, even in cross winds.

In 1946 another impressive machine appeared in the form of the 500cc ohv in-line twin Sunbeam, which had a fully-sprung frame and shaft drive. A 'car on two wheels', the Sunbeam featured rubber mounting of the power unit and oversize tyres to give a high standard of ride comfort.

However, there was still a considerable number of

Comfort was the keynote of the 1950 Sunbeam S7, with its fully-sprung frame and oversize tyres. Its in-line twin power unit was especially neat riders who wanted a modern version of the Ner-a-Car concept, a machine of moderate power that could be used by the non-enthusiast in all weathers.

To suit this section of the market, a remarkable 'Everyman' motor cycle was introduced by Velocette in 1948. Known as the LE, it had a 149cc water-cooled flat twin engine (later increased in size to 192cc) set transversely in a pressed steel frame, which incorporated legshields and ample mudguarding. An Olicana windshield on the handlebars gave almost complete weather protection to the rider. The silent running of this shaft-driven model made it a natural for police patrol work, and the 'Noddy bike' became a familiar sight on British roads over the next two decades.

Pioneer designer John Wooler, whose pre-First World War 'Flying Banana' had an ingenious horizontal flat-twin two-stroke engine using a double-ended piston to create crankcase compression, produced an even more unorthodox machine in 1948. Like its Edwardian ancestor, it had plunger suspension fore and aft and a fuel tank projecting forward of the steering head. There the resemblance ended, for the power unit was like nothing previously carried in a motor cycle frame.

It was nominally a flat-four, but had a bell-crank interposed between the four piston connecting rods and the connecting rod driving the single-throw crankshaft. It gave smooth running, but was short on performance. Also, the bottom frame tubes were used as exhaust pipes, which was not a good idea.

In 1953 Wooler tried again, with a more conventional 500cc flat-four, with shaft-drive and plunger suspension like its predecessor. It was a remarkable design, bristling with ingenious touches. Only three sizes of bolt were used throughout, and the toolbox was cast into the gearbox lid. It drew huge crowds at the 1954 show, but very few were made.

Somewhat similar in general appearance to the Wooler was the 350cc Douglas Dragonfly of 1954,

Mainstay of British police forces for a quarter-century – the silent and refined Velocette LE 'Noddy bike'

developed from a successfully unorthodox model of 1945 vintage, which had leading link hydraulically-damped front forks and torsion-bar rear-suspension. The Dragonfly had front and rear pivoted forks developed specially for Douglas by Reynolds Tubes, who were also responsible for the sturdy Duplex frame. The Dragonfly was one of the most handsome designs of its day. Unfortunately the increased preoccupation of its makers with the manufacture of Vespa scooters led to its demise a couple of years later.

A new variation on an old theme was the Triumph Speed Twin, which now incorporated a sprung rear hub replaced in 1954 by a pivoted rear fork. Like the LE Velocette, this model was popular with police forces, and examples were eventually in service all over the world.

Soon other manufacturers – AJS, Ariel, BSA, Matchless, Norton in England, Indian in the USA, and several Continental makers – featured at least one vertical twin in their ranges.

Last of the Douglas flat-twins was the handsome Dragonfly of 1954–56; the company had passed out of family control, and the boom in the scooters assembled by Douglas caused the end of motor cycle production

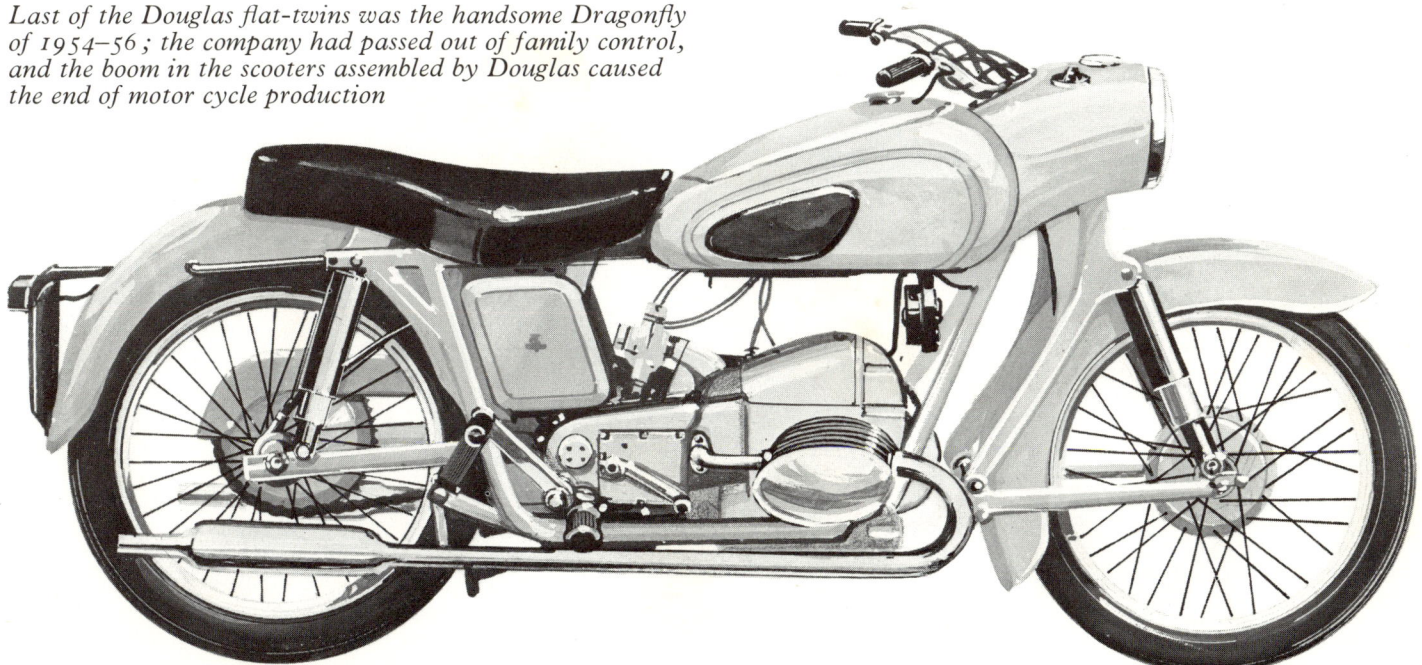

A complete break with the company's vee-twin tradition, the Harley Davidson SS 350 of 1969 (below) derived from their acquisition of the Italian Aer Macchi Company. It was a conscious attempt to design a European-type machine to compete with imported motor cycles

Yamaha began as makers of musical instruments like electronic organs, but proved equally as adept at producing fast motor cycles like this 1969 250cc D56 model (right)

Bridgestone's 1970 GTR 350 (opposite) had a six-speed gearbox and a rotary-valve two-stroke engine. It was good for over 100 mph. Even faster was the 130 mph BSA Rocket, with a 750 cc three-cylinder engine (opposite bottom); it failed to save its maker's crumbling fortunes

Even vertical twin two-strokes had become popular—Anzani made a 322cc power unit which Excelsior fitted in their Talisman Twin, while in 1958 Ariel combined a 249cc vertical two-stroke with an enclosed pressed-steel frame to produce the brilliant Leader, which was one of the first British machines to break away from traditional styling. It is an odd reflection on the taste of motor cyclists that the 'open' version of this machine, the Arrow, survived its streamlined brother in production.

Probably many motor cyclists who would have bought Leaders were wooed away by the increasing number of scooters which, from a handful produced

Full enclosure was the vogue of the late 1950s. Even police Triumphs (left) gained 'dustbin' fairings.
The unorthodox Ariel Leader of 1958, with its 250cc vertical twin two-stroke engine (below), had full weather protection built into its pressed steel frame

The growth of the scooter class after the Second World War was a phenomenon as inexplicable as the type's failure to catch on after the 1914–18 hostilities. A classic design of the times was the 1949 Piaggio Vespa (above), later built in England by Douglas. Less elegant – and less successful – was the contemporary Swallow Gadabout (right). It was built by the famous sidecar manufacturers and had a 122cc Villiers engine

just after the war, had grown to a positive deluge by the mid-1950s.

Although scooters had never really caught on after the First World War, in the post-World War Two years the type soon became accepted as practical. Much of the pioneering work had been done by the 98cc Corgi, developed from the wartime parachute-drop portable. It had 12·5in wheels and an ordinary bicycle saddle set atop a diminutive frame. In its three years of production (1945–8) a great many were sold.

Continental designers were more concerned with capturing the 'car-on-two-wheels' market than the average British manufacturer, so their most popular models featured full enclosure and weather protection. Italy was early in the field with two models destined to become classics of their kind: the Vespa, produced by the Piaggio Aircraft Company, and later made under licence in England by Douglas, and the Lambretta, built by Innocenti.

The scooter had a fantastic effect on the Italian motor cycle industry. From 1933 to 1950 – excluding, of course, the war – there were between 100 000 and 150 000 motor cycles in use in that country. In 1951 the figure suddenly quadrupled, it doubled again in 1952, and in 1953 it stood at 1 783 648, due almost entirely to the growth of the scooter market, which in 1953–4 represented almost 70 per cent of the value of the entire output of the Italian motor industry.

Built in Tonypandy, Glamorganshire, the Bown Autocycle represented British conservatism in an unsuccessful rearguard action against the scooters. It was powered by a 98cc JAP engine. Production ceased in the mid-1950s

More scooters and lightweights of the mid-1950s: the 1958 BSA Beezer (above) was an unsuccessful attempt to beat the Italians at their own game, while Douglas (left) merely joined them, and produced the highly successful Vespa. The Bond Sherpa (left, lower) was another unsuccessful British scooter, dating from 1956. The most popular of the early 50cc mopeds was the gawky NSU Quickly, seen below in 1956 'L' form

There was also an increase in the number of under 50cc outfits produced, either as complete machines or as 'clip-on' units for propelling pedal cycles. The best of the former type were machines like the German NSU Quickly; the latter including the British Mini-Motor and Winged Wheel and the Italian Ducati Cucciolo.

The majority of the clip-ons were single speed, often driving the cycle wheel by friction roller, but the Cucciolo was unusual on two counts. Firstly, its 49cc engine had overhead valves – tiny engines were normally two-strokes – and secondly its ribbed crankcase contained a train of gears, giving two speeds, with chain drive.

Most European countries – except Britain – allowed riders to run pedal-equipped 'mopeds' of below 50cc without needing to pass a driving test (the British law was subsequently relaxed to let car licence holders ride mopeds without passing a second driving test).

But if the average motorcylist was becoming increasingly interested in mounts of low capacity, 'big bangers' still dominated the sphere of competition.

One of the first new post war racers was unveiled in May 1947 by AJS. A remarkable 500cc double ohc parallel-twin, it had cylinders set at a slight angle to the horizontal. An odd feature was the cylinder-head, bristling with cooling spines rather than fins (a similar idea had been used on the veteran Knox cars in the USA); this earned the machine the nickname 'Porcupine'.

The Porcupine was certainly fast, and gained many competition successes, although the coveted Senior TT never came its way. It nearly won in 1949, in the able hands of Les Graham, but the magneto drive sheared on the last lap when it was virtually home and dry. By the time all the bugs had been sorted out, in 1954, the much-modified Porcupine was no match for the Nortons or the Italian racing fours.

Although Norton continued to enjoy their pre-war Senior TT winning streak in 1947, 1948 and 1949, it was clear that the time had come to pension off the old frame design in favour of something more capable of dealing with the increased output of the power unit.

The Irish brothers Cromie and Rex McCandless came up with the answer in 1949–50, working closely with the factory. Their 'Featherbed' frame had a full Duplex cradle layout, with hydraulically damped swinging fork rear suspension, and had a notably rigid steering head. The young rider Geoff Duke had the ability to exploit its superb handling to the full, and in 1950 scored his first Senior TT win at a record average of 92·27mph.

But the merits of the Featherbed frame were not lost on the Continental opposition, whose engines were far more potent than the Norton power unit.

Norton's designers were lulled into a false sense of security, thinking they could continue winning without the need to develop a faster engine. The Italian Gilera, introduced in 1948, had a transverse four-cylinder 500cc engine developing 55bhp, but its handling was poor. Then in 1953 Duke transferred his allegiance to Gilera, the handling problems were solved and he achieved a remarkable run of success, taking the world championship in 1953, 1954 and 1955.

The improvements to the design of the Gilera frame rendered the model virtually invincible in the mid-1950s. Apart from Duke's achievements, in the 1957 Golden Jubilee TT Races, Bob McIntyre won the Senior on a 500cc Gilera and the Junior on a 350cc version, the first time a foreign factory had achieved this coveted double. Not only that, but McIntyre raised

Heavy metal : the Featherbed-framed Manx Norton was the Birmingham company's racing swansong in the 1950s, although the reconstituted Norton firm made a modest return to the tracks in the 1970s

One of the racing aces of the late 1950s, who subsequently made the change to Grand Prix cars, was John Surtees, seen above riding the MV Agusta 500cc transverse four with which he dominated the racing scene in 1958–59–60. This was the first machine to achieve a 100mph average in the Manx TT

In contrast (right) this 1956 photo of a sidecar race shows the wide variety of machines, 'chairs' and riding positions then current

Rough-stuff riding is popular in both Old and New Worlds: contrast the exuberant style of Chuck Minert (left) on his BSA as he hurtles home to win the Los Angeles Catalina race of 1956, with the studied caution of Jeff Smith as he trickles a similar machine over an obstacle in the 1955 Scottish Six Days' Trial

the Senior lap record above the 100mph mark for the first time.

Leading rival of the Gilera was the Guzzi, with its distinctive triangulated space frame. It was available with a choice of horizontal single 350cc and 500cc engines and a 500cc four-in-line; unusually, the single proved more successful than the four.

In 1956 Guzzi introduced their *chef d'oeuvre* in the shape of an incredibly complex twin ohc 500cc vee-eight, with a maximum engine speed of 12 000 rpm, giving a top speed of more than 160mph. But it finished no higher than fourth in the 1957 Senior. Due to a

Complex and fast, the 1956 Guzzi V-8 (above) could reach 160mph at an engine speed of 12 000rpm, but its performance failed to live up to its promise

The classic four-cylinder MV Augusta (right) in 350cc form, ridden here by Carlo Bandirola. Les Graham placed a 500cc MV second in the 1952 Senior TT

The 350cc three-cylinder DKW of 1952–53 (below), with its oddly staggered cylinder layout, was another unorthodox machine. Right up to 1957 it led its class in road racing. The designer was Ing Erich Wolf

recession on the home market, the Italians then withdrew from racing.

Another odd cylinder layout was one that might be termed a 'vee-three', built in 1952 by the German DKW factory; it was a 350cc two-stroke, with 120 deg firing intervals for smooth running. It achieved several victories on the Continent, and was noted for its acceleration, due to its light weight (180lb dry) and capacity for revving (12 000rpm maximum).

In 1958, 1959 and 1960, the transverse four MV, another Italian machine, ruled the racing scene in England and on the Continent, generally with the redoubtable John Surtees at the helm. Surtees was the first rider to achieve a race average of 100mph in the Tourist Trophy. In 1961 this feat was equalled by Mike Hailwood riding a Manx Norton, the production racer built by Norton at their Bracebridge Street, Birmingham, works.

Norton had begun development of a 'four' to compete with Gilera, but this was shelved in 1954, when they dropped 'works' racing, even though their star rider, Ray Amm, had won the 1953 and 1954 Tourist Trophies, as well as setting up a new hour record of 133mph, all on streamlined versions of the old Manx single.

But Norton were in financial difficulties, and in 1962 the factory was taken over by Associated Motor Cycles Limited of London, and production of the Manx and development of its successor, the ohv twin Domiracer,

based on the production Dominator model, were stopped.

It was the beginning of the doldrums for the British motor cycle industry, even though total registrations had risen to virtually 2 000 000, a rise of 1 000 000 in ten years.

Part of the trouble was a growing difficulty for young riders, the main customers, to obtain insurance. Coupled with the growing availability of high-performance light cars, like the Mini, this meant that a considerable portion of the motor cycle market was switching its allegiance to four wheels. When the British Government brought in legislation limiting learner-riders to machines of under 250cc, the industry seemed lost. It had always promoted the big machines as the only ones worth bothering about – most of the British under-250s were presented as low-performance runabouts. The teenage learner wanted something more glamorous to hang his L plates from, and if the British manufacturers were not prepared to supply it, there were plenty of foreign companies able and willing to fill the gap in the market.

The initial sign of the changing times was the development of 'mini-motorbikes', notably by the Italians. Nominally mopeds, these machines featured huge tanks, megaphone exhaust systems and bright colour schemes.

Nor was the raciness always merely in the styling – the 1972 Casal moped from Portugal was capable of

Honda's C50 Moped of the early 1960s had a potent overhead valve 50cc engine which developed a remarkable 4·5 brake horsepower. Other features of the design were an automatic clutch and three-speed gearbox

This sporting lightweight is the Honda Motosport 90, which had an overhead camshaft single cylinder four-valve engine with a swept volume of 98·5cc and a power output of 8bhp at 9 000rpm. The duplex frame was an unusual item of specification for such a small machine

65mph, and caused a furore of apprehension when it seemed possible that the model might be imported into Britain!

But the biggest challenge to the world motor cycle industry was coming from the Far East, where Japan had been reconstituting war-shattered factories into hyper-efficient production units. The great success, of course, was Honda, founded in 1948 by Soichiro Honda, who bolted war-surplus two-stroke engines on to pedal cycles in a shack on a bomb site. In 1951, the Japanese industry turned out 11 354 motor cycles and 12 799 scooters, more than trebling these figures the next year. By 1960 Japan was making nearly 1 500 000 motor cycles and scooters annually, and, with a buoyant home market, moving confidently into the export field.

Japanese motor cycles first appeared in European competition in 1959 when a team of Hondas took the team prize in the 125cc TT with sixth, seventh, eighth and eleventh places. The next year they tried for the Lightweight honours with a 250cc transverse four. Then, in 1962 Honda swept the world championship board in the 125, 250 and 350cc classes. Other Japanese manufacturers, Yamaha and Suzuki, were soon racing seriously in Europe and it became apparent that the combination of top European riders and the speedy Japanese machines was a virtually unbeatable one.

An outstanding rider to emerge at this period was Mike Hailwood, son of a leading motor cycle dealer, who had started a brilliant racing career in the late 1950s at the age of seventeen. In 1962 he joined MV for an undisclosed sum, and until 1965 he was unbeatable in the 500cc class. Then he joined Honda as the highest-paid rider in the history of the sport, and notched up more remarkable successes, strongly challenged by one-time team-mate Giacomo Agostini (MV).

At the bottom end of the scale a 50cc TT had become part of the scene by the 1960s; the 1962 winner, Degner (Suzuki) averaged 75·12mph, faster than any vintage *Senior* winner!

This rapid expansion of the Japanese industry coincided with the beginnings of a remarkable trend, which was most evident in the United States–the increasing use of the motor cycle as a fun machine rather than a utilitarian means of transport.

The new customers were far removed from the traditional motorcyclist with his government surplus riding coat and beret and his propensity for breaking down at the roadside. They were car owners, successful and prosperous, looking for a machine that would recapture some of the lost excitement of their younger days. They wanted the best, and they were prepared to pay for it. The sophisticated features of the Japanese machines appealed to them. And the large-engined machines designed for these new enthusiasts acquired a new name–superbikes.

At first the British manufacturers tried their old tactics when something new appeared to be changing the market–ignore it, and hope it goes away. It was an attitude that had proved conspicuously disastrous in

the days of the scooter boom, but at least the scooters had eventually gone away. The Japanese, however, had far too much capital and technical know how invested to pull out of these new overseas markets. Instead, they piled on the pressure.

The British manufacturers just responded by making the same models they had been turning out for years.

Honda had moved into the British market in 1961. Their initial trump card was the 50cc Scooterette, a refined version of the old moped concept, with a four-stroke engine that made all other mopeds seem crude and noisy, plus ample weather protection. It caught on rapidly, and soon 8 000 a month were being sold.

The nearest thing Britain had to offer was the 125cc BSA Bantam, a utility motorcycle which was little different from pre-war models. One saw them all over the place ridden by Post Office messenger boys. Minor styling alterations did nothing to help the Bantam's plebeian image. Honda's 50cc model creamed off the utilitarian end of the market, while their lightweight motorcycles were so attractive that the British machines were rapidly squeezed out.

For instance, the Honda CB 72 Sports 250 of the early 1960s was a distinctively styled twin with a backbone frame. It featured an electric starter, which British manufacturers regarded as an effeminate affectation–surely all red-blooded motor cyclists enjoyed kick starting their mounts?–yet despite its comprehensive equipment it could top 90mph. Its nearest British equivalent, the 250cc BSA Sports Star, was a vertical single capable of only 70mph.

Before long, more Hondas were being sold in Britain than all other makes combined. Japanese annual output broke the 2 000 000 mark in 1964, and hovered just under 2 500 000 during the later part of the decade. Over half this production went for export, predominately to the USA, which bought 266 092 Japanese motor cycles, mostly over 50cc–Honda experienced tremendous marketing problems with their moped range in America in 1966 through over-saturation of the dealerships–and to Vietnam, where 282 615 mopeds were sold in the same period. The main European buyer of Japanese two-wheelers was Britain, which took 74 418 in 1968.

The first casualty of the Japanese onslaught was Associated Motor Cycles, initially formed as a protective umbrella for companies affected by the harmful publicity given by the leather-clad coffee-bar cowboys of the late 1950s.

The anti-social behaviour of the cowboys, real and fictional, caused a major slump in sales of the larger machines. 'United we stand' might have been the motto of AMC, which took in AJS, Matchless, Norton, James and Francis-Barnett, plus the Villiers and JAP engine companies. But the reorganisation programme came too late, and was too limited in scope, and in the early 1960s AMC collapsed.

The remnants were acquired by the Manganese Bronze industrial group, and reconstituted as Norton-Villiers, building almost exclusively under the Norton trademark. A decade later Manganese Bronze also took over the remains of the ailing BSA company.

In late 1967 Norton announced a new model for the superbike market, the 750cc Commando (which actually went on sale in 1968). Its vertical-twin engine was a far from new design, and customers and critics alike were at first sceptical about the manufacturer's claims that the new frame and Isolastic rubber engine mountings would eliminate vibration. But Norton were proved right. Although the engine still vibrated, the rubber mountings proved remarkably effective, and the overall effect was that from the rider's point of view the Commando was uncannily smooth.

As Norton-Villiers chairman Dennis Poore subsequently commented: 'We don't see the advantage of the complication of three and four cylinder engines when you can get similar results by other means'.

The latest variant on the Commando theme is the 1973 Interstate, fitted with the high-compression Combat engine which develops 65bhp, making this the most powerful road-going Norton ever produced, with a top speed potential of 120mph plus. Allied to this performance is super stopping power provided by a 10·7 inch front disc brake with hydraulic operation.

The production racer version of the Commando is capable of developing 72bhp, and for the first time since the closure of Bracebridge Street, a Norton works team has appeared on racing circuits, with this machine.

But if Norton have managed to pull round, with 1972 turnover up 60 percent over the previous year, for the biggest British manufacturer, BSA-Triumph the 1970s opened in an atmosphere of crisis. In 1970 it seemed that BSA-Triumph was on the point of a return to power, with a range of superbikes such as the well-tried Triumph Bonneville 650cc twin and the newer BSA/Triumph three-cylinder 750cc machines. These were prime export models – in 1969 a BSA Rocket Three set up nine records in America from 5 miles (131·7mph), 200 miles (123·1mph), lapping with chronometric consistency – in a whole new range.

Suddenly the bottom dropped out of BSA's market. Many of the new machines never reached production stage, and the group's £1 250 000 profits became a £2 500 000 loss. Barclays Bank stepped in to plug the gap with a £10 000 000 loan, backed up by £5 000 000 raised by the company. The range was cut to the bare minimum, and even the 50cc bicycle that was the last bearer of the once proud name of Ariel fell under the axe.

The well-tried twin and triple-cylinder models were the mainstay of the revised BSA-Triumph lineup. Customers for the three-cylinder 750cc models could choose between the traditionally styled Trident or a way-out version, the X-75 Hurricane, designed by Illinois artist Craig Vetter. With a five-speed transmission, the Hurricane had a pop-art tank/seat unit and fan-shaped triple megaphone exhausts, and was aimed principally at the American market.

The root cause of the problem was apparent from the teetering sales graphs of previous years: from a record 171 700 motor cycles produced by British makers in 1951, the figure had fallen to a low of 51 000 by

Superbikes of the seventies: a water-cooled three-cylinder engine (top) was an unusual feature of the 1972 Suzuki 750 WC-Three, while Kawasaki brought out the world's most powerful motor cycle, this 900cc transverse four (above) for the 1973 season. Most expensive roadburner, though, was the £2000 MV 750 four of the same year (below), with a design firmly based on racing experience

Honda's CB 500 (top) was just one of that company's transverse fours; electric starting and disc brakes were part of the specification. The 1973 Honda range also included this neat 350cc transverse four (above). Biggest motor cycle currently produced in Europe is the massive Munch Mammut, a 1200cc transverse four with a complex power unit (below)

1963. Moped production had dropped from a record 78 800 in 1959 to 10 774 in 1968; scooter output had plummeted even more drastically, from 30 000 in 1961 to a mere 28 in 1968.

In 1958 there had been forty British motor cycle manufacturers: in 1972 the figure had dropped to around 10, with the majority of these building on a limited scale, like Scott, Cotton and Velocette.

However, the outlook was not unreservedly gloomy. During the decade 1958–1968, exports rose from 36 559 to 65 887, increasing in value from £4 835 500 to £16 550 000.

A new internationalism had some surprising feedbacks, among which was the revival of the old Royal Enfield name, carried by a robust little 175cc two-stroke designed to meet police and Auto Cycle Union training requirements. But the modern Royal Enfield is produced a long way from its traditional home in Redditch; most of the manufacture is carried out in the Enfield India factory in Madras, with final assembly at the Norton works at Andover, Hampshire.

While home established names were making a comeback, new ones appeared. In 1972 W.E. Wassell of Walsall–probably the biggest motor cycle component maker in Britain–announced their entry into machine production with a range of competition motor cycles powered by the 125cc German Sachs engine.

Worldwide, motorcycle registration figures were remarkable: over 5 000 000 machines were sold in 1972. Most of the sales were of 'sensible' commuter machines, but there were plenty of superbikes among them.

Typical of the new breed of superbike was the 1970 Bridgestone GTR350, built by Japan's biggest tyre maker. It had a 350cc twin-cylinder two-stroke engine with rotary inlet valves, and a six-speed transmission. Its top speed was 103mph and it could cover a standing quarter-mile in under 14 seconds.

Suzuki, originally manufacturers of weaving machinery, entered the motor cycle field in 1952, concentrating on the development of two-stroke engines, with pressure lubrication rather than petroil.

The 1972 Suzuki range covered the entire spectrum from the F50 moped to 120mph superbikes. Stars of the line-up were three three-cylinder models–the GT380J six-speeder and the GT550J five-speeder, both with Suzuki's novel ram-air-cooling system, and the five-speed GT750J, with the unusual feature of water-cooling.

Like Honda Suzuki believed in a policy of improving the breed through racing. So did Yamaha, makers of musical instruments, whose first motor cycle appeared in 1955. Among the features of their machines are five-speed gearboxes to get the optimum performance from their high-revving power units.

In 1972 Yamaha announced their first road-going 500cc model, the 7X 500, with a twin-cylinder engine incorporating a double-overhead camshaft and four valves per cylinder. Electric starting and front disc brakes were standard. It was a fitting stablemate for their other big parallel twin the 650cc XSZ.

In 1968 Honda topped the superbike market with a

four-cylinder model based on their racing machines. It had a 750cc engine and a five-speed gearbox; electric starting and disc brakes (the first fitted to a mass production machine) were featured in the specification. Maximum speed was in the region of 125mph. This was perhaps the most sophisticated touring motor cycle then marketed and even at its price of $1 100 in Japan, inflated by import duty to £670 in the United Kingdom, the CB 750 enjoyed ready sales. Up to 100mph, nothing on four wheels short of a Lamborghini Miura could outperform the Honda.

Also based on racing know-how was the Kawasaki Mach III, a 498cc two-stroke three-cylinder with a 120mph top speed and a 0–100mph time of 12·5sec, faster than the majority of sports cars. It had transistorised ignition, needing no contact breaker, and the sparking plugs were self-cleaning, removing one of the traditional bogies of two-stroke design.

In the superbike field, Kawasaki first rivalled Honda with the introduction of a 750, then completely stole their thunder with the transverse four, double overhead camshaft 900cc model Z1 of 1972, the most powerful motor cycle in production, developing 82bhp. This gave the Kawasaki a top speed of over 125mph, coupled

with ability to cover a standing start quarter mile in 12 seconds.

A glimpse of the superbike of tomorrow was given at the 1972 Tokyo Show, where Yamaha unveiled the first ever motor cycle powered by a Wankel rotary engine. With a water-cooled twin-rotor engine developing 68bhp linked to a five-speed gearbox, the RZ 201 promised to be an exciting performer.

Following a tradition of advanced engineering, Germany continued to make ultra refined motor cycles. For instance, the NSU Max of the mid-1950s featured eccentric drive to the overhead camshaft, rather than the more common shaft or gears. BMW continued to refine the old ABC theme, coming up with an entirely

Latest development of the BMW theme is the 1970 R75, with its 745cc flat-twin engine. The general layout still follows the pattern laid down by the first BMWs in 1923; for many years after the war BMW was Germany's sole manufacturer of over 250cc motor cycles

new range of shaft-driven flat-twins for 1970. Largest of these new models was the electrically-started 745cc R75, which incorporated many features developed on BMW's car range. Silent and refined, the big BMW was also heavy (436lb ready to go), expensive and fast, with a top speed of 103mph.

Nearly twice the capacity of this big BMW was the limited-production Munch Mammut, a 1 200 cc transverse-four, the largest-engined motor cycle in production in Europe.

At the other end of the capacity scale, French production was almost exclusively of under 50cc cyclomoteurs, of which 1 120 329 were turned out in 1968; only a few thousand 'real' motor cycles were made in that year.

Italian cyclemotor production continued to rise, too, from 205 000 in 1962 to 540 000 in 1968, but annual production of lightweights and scooters under 125cc dropped from 210 000 to 61 000 over the same period, while over 125cc machines fell from 198 000 to 90 600. Styling remained a striking feature of Italian design, with mopeds endowed with massive racing tanks, dropped handlebars, and other sporting appurtenances, five and six-speed gearboxes being a feature of several 1970 models.

The Italians had not forgotten how to make high-performance big bikes. The Guzzi V7 was a 760cc transverse vee-twin capable of developing 68bhp in tuned form, and in 1969 one of these machines averaged 134mph for an hour to set up a new world

record. MV provided the most expensive machine at the 1972 London Motorcycle Show–a new version of their 750cc race-bred transverse four, bearing a shattering £2 000-plus price tag.

In the spiritual home of the superbikes, the United States, Harley-Davidson had continued production of big vee-twins which were simultaneously favoured by police and Hell's Angels.

Italian design played its part in the American industry too, for Harley-Davidson acquired the Italian Aermacchi concern with a view to finding out what made European motor cycles tick. Harley's 1969 SS350 was recognisably derived from European trends, with its massive, almost horizontal, single-cylinder engine.

European influence of a different kind was displayed in revived Indian models appearing in the late 1960s, which used 750cc Royal Enfield and 500cc Velocette power units, in Italian-engineered frames. The Indian story had become a sad one after the war, when the moribund Indian Motocycle Company had been acquired by the British Brockhouse Corporation, who produced a range of Indian Brave lightweights which had nothing in common with the great Hendee designs; subsequently the name was acquired by publisher Floyd Clymer, who produced the new models.

In America in the late 1960s there was a growing vogue for high-performance off-road motor cycles, which were developed in machine-breaking marathon endurance runs. The boom in the new type of sporting motor cycles led to the construction of some interesting new models.

The Spanish Bultaco company, founded in a barnyard in 1958 to build lightweights, was soon established as makers of first-rate sports and racing machines. In 1965 Bultaco brought out a high-performance motocross model, the Pursang-Métisse, which combined a 36bhp 250cc two-stroke engine and the trials-proven Rickman-Metisse frame. Bultaco's 1968 El Bandido motocross mount was even more spectacular, with 360cc developing 43·5bhp. Demand for Bultaco's wide range of sporting and racing lightweights was such that in 1966 sales passed the 20 000 mark–and a third of these went to the USA.

Among other leading makers of off-road motor cycles was the Swedish Husqvarna, long established as makers of sporting two-wheelers. Their 1970 offering was a 250cc eight-speed motocross model, with a single-cylinder six-port two-stroke engine.

After analysing the construction and handling of a number of outstanding off-road machines, Kawasaki evolved the 346cc F5 Bighorn for 1970. This had Hatta front forks, incorporating a remarkable degree of adjustment, with provision for variation of caster angle, rake and wheelbase, and with seven-inch fork travel, adjustments which made the Bighorn suitable for all types of off-road use, as well as for normal road riding. A light but strong duplex frame and five-speed unit gearbox were features of this machine.

By the early 1950s scrambling–racing over a rough, muddy track–had grown to be a major spectator sport in Europe, dominated by British and Swedish riders.

Moto-cross is just the latest name for the old motor cycle sport of mud-plugging—but now it's big business . . .

Astute television coverage helped swell the attraction of this blood and guts sport, now generally known by its European title of moto-cross, which gains its attraction from the spectacle of man and machine battling for supremacy on atrocious terrain. Such is the appeal of moto-cross that two of the leading makers of scrambles bikes have become major figures in the British motor cycle industry. Greeves, especially, who are now the third biggest makers, are a force to be reckoned with. And the Rickman brothers' *Métisse* (mongrel bitch) models were originally built as one-off specials utilising Triumph Tiger 498cc power units in BSA Gold Star frames. By 1972 Rickman had become so much part of the motor cycle establishment that they were offering a Triumph twin engined police mount and a 125cc Zundapp-powered replacement for the old Velocette 'Noddybike'.

In the 1970s, Norton-Villiers revived the honoured AJS name for the Stormer off-road machines. In December 1970 Californian Doug Douglas rode an AJS Stormer 250 from Tijuana to La Paz—1000 miles of desert, mountains and scrub across Mexico—in 27 hours 11 minutes, trimming 11 hours 39 minutes off the existing record. In 1972 a larger Stormer, the 410 with a 35bhp engine, was introduced.

The motor cycle story has shown a remarkable evolution. While the interest in the sporting side has remained remarkably consistent, with rallies and trials organised in much the same way that they have always been, the image of the roadgoing bike has changed completely.

There will always be the low-price utility mount, but even this now benefits from the improved image of the bigger machines.

With performance and styling predominant factors, the superbikes have sloughed off the old utilitarian concept of motorcycling, and these exhilarating machines have given the once maligned two-wheeler a glamour lacking since the heyday of the Vincent and the Brough Superior.

From the way the sales graphs are soaring, it looks as though the new image is here to stay.

Index